HOW TO START A
TRAVEL AGENCY

A Comprehensive Guide to Starting, Running and Growing a Profitable Travel Business

CURTIS POWERS

Copyright Notice

This book is copyrighted in 2019-2024 by Dan & Elbert Associates.

All rights reserved.
Its content may not be copied or duplicated in part or whole by any means without express prior agreement in writing

TABLE OF CONTENTS

Introduction   5
    Overview of the Travel Industry   6
    The Growing Demand for Personalized Travel Experiences   8
    Why Start a Travel Agency   11

Chapter 1: Defining Your Vision and Niche   13
    Choosing Your Niche   15
    Setting Your Vision and Mission   17

Chapter 2: Market Research and Feasibility Study   21
    Identifying Target Markets   21
    Analyzing Competitors   23
    Assessing Industry Trends   26

Chapter 3: Creating a Business Plan   31
    Executive Summary   31
    Company Description   32
    Market Research and Target Audience   33
    Competitive Analysis   35
    Marketing and Sales Strategy   37
    Service Offerings and Operations Plan   40
    Financial Plan and Projections   41
    Risk Management and Contingency Plan   43

Chapter 4: Legal Requirements and Certifications   47
    Licensing and Registration   47
    Obtaining Industry Certifications   51
    Travel Insurance and Liability   54

Chapter 5: Building Partnerships and Supplier Relationships   **59**

    Working with Travel Suppliers   59

    Developing a Global Network   65

    Negotiating Commission and Compensation Models   68

Chapter 6: Creating a Marketing Strategy   **73**

    Building Your Brand   73

    Designing a User-Friendly Website   75

    Social Media and Content Marketing   78

    Paid Advertising and SEO   82

Chapter 7: Managing Operations and Customer Experience   **87**

    Booking Systems and Software   87

    Providing Excellent Customer Service   90

    Handling Complaints and Emergencies   92

Chapter 8: Scaling Your Travel Agency   **95**

    Expanding Your Services   95

    Hiring and Training Staff   98

    Leveraging Technology for Growth   100

Conclusion   **107**

Introduction

Starting a travel agency is more than just creating itineraries and booking flights—it's about crafting unforgettable experiences and making travel dreams a reality. With the global travel industry evolving rapidly, the opportunities to create a unique, customer-centric agency are greater than ever. From specialized travel niches and personalized customer service to using cutting-edge technology, today's travel agencies offer a blend of expertise, convenience, and adventure that travelers value deeply.

This book, How to Start a Travel Agency: A Comprehensive Guide, provides a step-by-step blueprint for building a successful travel agency from the ground up. Whether you're passionate about connecting people to cultures worldwide, helping families make memories, or introducing corporate clients to stress-free business travel, this guide covers everything you need to know to get started and grow.

You'll learn how to identify a profitable niche, develop a strategic business plan, build strong industry partnerships, and market your services effectively in a competitive landscape. The chapters also dive into key aspects like setting up efficient operations, managing finances, and creating a brand that resonates with your target audience. In addition, you'll explore ways to adapt to industry trends, from digital innovations to eco-conscious travel, and how to stay ahead in a fast-changing market.

Whether you're starting a home-based agency, opening a storefront, or venturing into online travel services, this guide empowers you to build a resilient business focused on delivering exceptional travel experiences. By combining tried-and-true strategies with modern approaches, you'll be equipped to transform your passion for travel into a profitable, rewarding career. Let's embark on this journey together, turning your vision into a thriving travel agency!

Overview of the Travel Industry

Travel agencies provide essential services that make the travel process seamless, enjoyable, and accessible. At their core, they act as intermediaries between travelers and various travel-related services, such as airlines, hotels, car rental companies, and tour operators. They offer expertise in planning itineraries, booking flights, arranging accommodations, and coordinating ground transportation, allowing clients to focus solely on enjoying their trip. Travel agents use their industry knowledge and relationships to secure better deals and ensure clients get the best value for their money. This saves clients hours of research, reduces the stress of trip planning, and provides peace of mind that their journey is well-organized.

Beyond handling logistics, travel agencies personalize travel experiences based on clients' interests, budgets, and travel goals. They listen closely to clients' needs to craft custom itineraries, whether for a romantic getaway, family vacation, luxury experience, or business trip. This personalized approach has become increasingly valuable in a world where online booking platforms offer cookie-cutter options. Travel agents consider clients' preferences, offering unique recommendations like hidden-gem accommodations, local tour guides, or experiences that align with personal interests, ensuring a trip that feels tailored to the traveler rather than a generic package.

Travel agencies also serve as problem solvers and safety nets for their clients. In cases of unforeseen circumstances, such as flight delays, cancellations, lost baggage, or emergency situations, travel agents can quickly provide solutions and alternatives. They often have access to industry contacts and insider information that allow them to navigate these issues with speed and efficiency, ensuring clients experience minimal disruptions. Having a dedicated travel agent to handle such issues can be invaluable, especially when clients are in unfamiliar locations or dealing with language barriers.

Moreover, travel agencies provide access to exclusive deals and promotions through established partnerships with travel service providers. These partnerships can allow agents to offer discounts, upgrades, or VIP services not accessible through typical booking platforms. Some agencies even specialize in particular types of travel, such as luxury, eco-tourism, or destination weddings, further elevating their clients' experiences. For corporate clients, travel agencies often provide comprehensive management services, helping businesses coordinate travel for employees, negotiate rates with hotels and airlines, and ensure adherence to company travel policies.

In addition to these services, many travel agencies stay current with travel trends, regulatory changes, and health and safety requirements, providing clients with updated information and advice. Especially in today's environment, where travel restrictions and guidelines are constantly changing, having a knowledgeable travel agent can alleviate concerns about compliance and logistics. From obtaining visas to advising on vaccination requirements or local customs, travel agencies prepare clients for all aspects of their journey, making their travel experience both enjoyable and worry-free.

Travel agencies create value by turning travel dreams into reality, guiding clients through the entire travel process with convenience, reliability, and expertise. By combining their professional networks, industry knowledge, and passion for creating memorable journeys, they provide a unique and essential service in the world of travel.

The digital age has revolutionized nearly every aspect of the travel business. Online travel agencies (OTAs), social media platforms, and mobile apps have transformed how consumers discover, plan, and book their vacations. Today, travelers have instant access to endless choices at their fingertips, from flights and accommodations to personalized tours and experiences. This shift has led to a highly competitive market, but it has also opened doors for travel agencies that focus on offering highly curated and personalized services.

Understanding the role of technology in the travel industry is key to building a successful agency. While digital platforms allow consumers to self-book trips, they often lack the expertise and human touch that a specialized travel agency can provide. As an agency owner, your ability to offer tailored experiences, one-on-one consultation, and expert recommendations will set you apart from the digital giants.

Technology can also work in your favor. With advancements in booking software, customer relationship management (CRM) systems, and marketing automation tools, travel agents today have access to resources that make running a business more efficient and scalable. These tools can streamline your operations, allow you to build relationships with clients, and enhance the overall travel experience.

The Growing Demand for Personalized Travel Experiences
One of the most significant trends shaping the travel industry today is the increasing demand for personalized experiences. As travelers become more discerning and adventurous, they are actively seeking out journeys that resonate with their individual tastes, preferences, and lifestyles. Gone are the days of cookie-cutter vacation packages; today's travelers want curated itineraries that reflect their unique interests, hobbies, and aspirations. Whether

it's a wellness retreat aimed at rejuvenation, a luxury cruise offering opulent experiences, or an eco-friendly adventure that aligns with their values, people are looking for trips that transcend the typical tourist experience.

This shift toward personalization presents a tremendous opportunity for travel agencies willing to specialize and tailor their services. Instead of attempting to cater to a broad audience, successful travel agents are increasingly narrowing their focus to specific niches within the industry. By concentrating on areas such as luxury travel, destination weddings, adventure tourism, or corporate travel, agents not only position themselves as experts but also foster deeper connections with their target audience. Specialization allows you to cultivate a rich understanding of your chosen niche, enabling you to provide insights and recommendations that resonate with clients on a personal level.

Your travel agency can become the key to unlocking exclusive experiences for your clients. By establishing strong relationships with suppliers, hoteliers, tour operators, and local guides, you can offer insider access to special events, hidden gems, and off-the-beaten-path destinations that travelers would never discover on their own. This insider knowledge not only enhances the travel experience but also sets your agency apart in a crowded market. In a world where travelers are bombarded with information and options, providing these personalized services can significantly impact their decision-making process, making your agency their go-to resource for travel planning.

Moreover, personalization goes beyond simply tailoring itineraries; it extends to understanding your clients on a deeper level. Engaging with clients to learn about their travel history, preferences, and future aspirations can help you craft experiences that resonate with them personally. This attention to detail can transform a regular trip into a memorable journey that exceeds expectations. For instance, if a client expresses an interest in culinary experiences, you can recommend cooking classes with local chefs, food tours in vibrant markets, or exclusive dining opportunities that reflect the destination's culture. By integrating these elements into your offerings, you not only enhance the travel experience but also build lasting relationships with your clients.

In addition, leveraging technology can further enhance the personalization of travel experiences. Utilizing customer relationship management (CRM) systems allows you to track client interactions, preferences, and feedback, enabling you to offer customized recommendations based on their past travel experiences. This data-driven approach can enhance the efficiency of your services while making clients feel valued and understood. Furthermore, the rise of artificial intelligence and chatbots can provide immediate assistance to clients, helping them explore options and answer questions in real-time, thus creating a seamless booking experience.

In conclusion, the growing demand for personalized travel experiences reflects a broader shift in consumer behavior, where travelers seek meaningful and tailored adventures. For travel agencies willing to specialize and focus on building strong relationships with clients and suppliers, this trend offers a unique opportunity for differentiation and growth. By curating unforgettable experiences that align with clients' interests and values, your agency can stand out as a trusted partner in their journey. In an increasingly crowded travel landscape, the ability to provide personalized services will not only attract clients but also foster loyalty and repeat business, ultimately contributing to the long-term success of your travel agency.

Why Start a Travel Agency

Starting a travel agency offers a unique blend of business opportunity and personal fulfillment. For those who have a deep love for exploring new places, cultures, and experiences, creating a business that allows you to share that passion with others can be incredibly rewarding. Unlike many industries, travel is all about connecting people to the world around them, helping clients fulfill lifelong dreams, or simply making complex travel arrangements easier. If you're someone who finds joy in helping others plan, explore, and enjoy meaningful trips, a travel agency can be the perfect business to harness that enthusiasm into a profitable career.

The travel industry is vast and constantly evolving, offering endless opportunities for innovation and specialization. Starting a travel agency allows you to tap into niche markets, whether in luxury travel, adventure tours, eco-tourism, or family vacations. By specializing in a specific type of travel, you can set your agency apart from the big online platforms, offering personalized service, unique itineraries, and expert advice that larger companies often can't provide. This specialization creates loyal clients who trust your expertise and will return to you for future trips, appreciating the value of a customized, hands-on experience.

Additionally, running a travel agency offers flexibility that many other business models do not. Modern travel agencies can operate from a physical office, but many successful agencies today are fully digital, allowing owners and employees to work remotely. This opens up opportunities to work from anywhere in the world while staying connected to your clients. It also makes it possible to start a home-based agency with lower overhead costs, making it an appealing option for those looking to start a business on a budget. With digital tools, virtual meetings, and online booking systems, you can operate a professional agency without the need for a storefront.

Financially, a travel agency can be a lucrative venture with multiple revenue streams. Agencies earn income through commissions, booking fees, partnerships with airlines and hotels, and added-value services like travel insurance or customized itineraries. With a growing demand for curated travel experiences, travelers are often willing to pay for the expertise and convenience that a knowledgeable travel agent brings to the table. This demand is especially strong among certain demographics, such as families looking for stress-free vacation planning, luxury travelers desiring exclusive experiences, and corporations seeking managed travel solutions.

Finally, a travel agency is not just a business; it's a role that lets you become a trusted adviser, guiding clients to new destinations, creating memories, and even transforming lives. When clients return with stories of life-changing trips, you know you've made a lasting impact. For those who thrive on personal connections and want to make a difference in people's lives, running a travel agency is not just profitable but profoundly fulfilling. By turning your love for travel into a business, you gain the opportunity to share that joy with others, foster a loyal customer base, and build a business that can grow as you do.

Chapter 1:
Defining Your Vision and Niche

The travel industry is one of the most diverse, dynamic, and expansive sectors in the global economy. From tourism to business trips, adventure travel to luxury vacations, the industry caters to a broad spectrum of traveler needs. It serves people seeking experiences in faraway lands, as well as those requiring simple arrangements for routine business travel. Understanding this complex and multifaceted industry is crucial when you embark on the journey of starting a travel agency.

The first step in defining your travel agency's vision and niche is gaining a thorough understanding of the travel industry as a whole. This sector encompasses various services and activities, including transportation (airlines, cruise lines, trains), accommodation (hotels, resorts, vacation rentals), tour operators, travel agents, and activities or experiences such as guided tours, events, and cultural experiences. Additionally, the industry touches on adjacent areas like insurance, technology, food and beverage, and wellness services, as these are often integral to travel experiences.

A closer look reveals that the industry can be broken down into distinct categories. Leisure travel is one of the largest segments, comprising vacations, holidays, honeymoons, and other trips taken for pleasure. This segment is driven by people's desire to explore new destinations, relax, or experience different cultures. Whether it's a budget-friendly backpacking trip or a high-end luxury escape, the variety of options within leisure travel is immense.

On the other hand, corporate travel is an entirely different beast, centered on the needs of business professionals who travel for work. These trips often require streamlined booking processes, flexible schedules, and specific services, such as meeting and conference arrangements, group travel, and executive accommodations. Corporate travelers typically prioritize convenience, efficiency, and reliability, making this sector highly service-oriented.

Another rapidly growing area is specialized travel services, which cater to specific types of trips like destination weddings, medical tourism, educational trips, or sports tourism. Each specialized segment has its unique demands and requires tailored knowledge and offerings. For example, destination wedding planners need to understand not only the logistics of travel but also legal requirements, local traditions, and venue arrangements.

Within this vast ecosystem, adventure tourism is another exciting segment that is growing in popularity. As travelers increasingly seek immersive experiences that push their boundaries, adventure travel agencies can offer guided treks, extreme sports, wildlife safaris, or eco-friendly expeditions. This sector often appeals to thrill-seekers and nature enthusiasts and requires in-depth knowledge of specific regions and activities.

The rise of eco-tourism and sustainable travel reflects broader societal trends toward environmental consciousness and responsible travel. Eco-tourism focuses on promoting travel that minimizes environmental impact and supports local communities, which is becoming more popular among environmentally conscious travelers. In this niche, your knowledge of conservation efforts, sustainable practices, and how to reduce the carbon footprint of travel will be essential.

In addition to these broad categories, destination-specific services are another area to explore. Agencies that specialize in a particular country, region, or even city offer clients in-depth knowledge and access to exclusive experiences. For instance, a travel agency specializing in African safaris will have established relationships with local guides, accommodations, and tour providers that a general travel agency may lack.

As a prospective travel agency owner, it's essential to assess where your strengths lie and which part of this broad industry you're most passionate about. By developing a comprehensive understanding of the various travel segments, you can begin to identify opportunities that align with your skills, experience, and business goals.

Choosing Your Niche

Once you've gained a broad understanding of the travel industry, the next critical step is to choose your niche. In such a competitive field, it's crucial to distinguish yourself from the multitude of online travel platforms, agencies, and tour operators. Defining a niche allows you to target a specific audience and offer them tailored services that set you apart as an expert. Whether you're passionate about eco-friendly adventures or corporate travel solutions, honing in on a niche will help you carve out a space in the marketplace.

Choosing the right niche involves several considerations. What are you passionate about? If you're an avid adventurer with a deep love for nature and wildlife, perhaps eco-tourism or adventure travel could be your niche. On the other hand, if you've always had a fascination with luxury hotels and exclusive resorts, then focusing on high-end leisure travel may be the best fit. What are your areas of expertise? Your experience and knowledge in specific travel destinations, activities, or types of travel can help you decide on your niche.

It's also important to consider the market demand for your chosen niche. Do your research to identify trends and opportunities in the industry. For example, eco-tourism is seeing significant growth due to rising environmental awareness among travelers. The COVID-19 pandemic has also driven an increase in domestic and local travel, as people opt for road trips or "staycations" over international travel. Additionally, luxury travel continues to grow as affluent travelers seek out exclusive, unique, and high-end experiences that cater to their desires.

Specialization can also come from targeting a specific demographic. For instance, there is a rising demand for family-friendly travel, with parents seeking vacation packages that cater to children of different age groups. Solo travelers, particularly women, are another demographic that has seen growth, prompting travel agencies to offer packages with enhanced safety measures, personalized itineraries, and group travel options.

You might also choose to focus on niche markets such as LGBTQ+ travel, accessible travel for individuals with disabilities, or religious tourism. Each of these markets has unique needs, and by developing a deep understanding of these clients, you can offer tailored services that address their specific requirements.

Another factor to consider when selecting your niche is the competition. Some niches, like general leisure travel, are highly saturated. Competing with large online platforms and well-established agencies can be difficult. However, narrowing your focus to an underserved or specialized niche allows you to become a leader in that area. For example, if you focus solely on wellness retreats that include yoga, meditation, and spa experiences, you can build a reputation as the go-to agency for those seeking rejuvenating travel.

Technology and trends should also influence your decision. The rise of digital nomads—individuals who work remotely while traveling—has created demand for long-term stays, co-working spaces, and unique accommodations that cater to professionals on the move. If you have an interest in this growing market, creating travel packages and services that cater to digital nomads can differentiate your agency.

Once you've chosen your niche, you'll need to develop a comprehensive understanding of that specific market. If you've chosen to specialize in destination weddings, for example, you'll need to be well-versed in legal requirements, local customs, venue options, and partner vendors in your chosen destinations. You'll also need to stay informed about trends and changes within your niche. Clients will expect you to provide expert advice, which means constantly expanding your knowledge and building relationships with key partners.

Ultimately, your niche will define the direction of your business and help shape your brand identity. It will influence your marketing strategy, partnerships, and service offerings. A well-chosen niche not only distinguishes you from the competition but also helps you develop a loyal customer base that values your expertise. Travelers are more likely to choose an agency that deeply understands their needs over a generalized service, especially when they are seeking a unique or complex travel experience.

Setting Your Vision and Mission

Your vision and mission are the guiding principles that will define the direction and purpose of your travel agency. They serve as the foundation for everything from business decisions to client relationships. A clear vision outlines what you aspire to achieve, while your mission focuses on how you will deliver on that vision. Together, they form the heart of your brand and influence every aspect of your business, from customer service to marketing.

Your vision statement should be aspirational. It reflects the ultimate goal of your travel agency and the impact you want to make in the industry. Ask yourself, what do you want your agency to be known for? How do you want to shape the experiences of your clients? Your vision might focus on becoming the go-to agency for exclusive, once-in-a-lifetime luxury vacations, or it could emphasize creating sustainable, eco-friendly travel options that benefit local communities.

For example, if you're passionate about adventure travel, your vision could be: "To inspire and empower travelers to explore the world's most breathtaking landscapes and push their limits through unforgettable, sustainable adventures." This vision reflects both your focus on adventure and your commitment to responsible travel practices.

On the other hand, if your focus is on corporate travel, your vision might be: "To be the leading provider of seamless and efficient corporate travel solutions, ensuring that every business trip is productive, stress-free, and tailored to meet the unique needs of professionals." This clearly communicates your intent to dominate the corporate travel space by offering exceptional service and support.

Once you've established your vision, the next step is to define your mission statement. Your mission should describe the practical steps you will take to achieve your vision. It's the "how" behind your business goals and reflects your values and the experience you aim to deliver to your clients.

For instance, if your agency focuses on eco-tourism, your mission might be: "To provide environmentally conscious travel experiences that connect travelers with nature while supporting local communities and promoting sustainable practices." This mission communicates your agency's commitment to eco-friendly travel and the specific actions you will take to achieve that goal, such as supporting local businesses or partnering with conservation organizations.

If your agency specializes in luxury travel, your mission could be: "To curate bespoke, high-end travel experiences that exceed client expectations by providing exceptional service, exclusive access to elite destinations, and personalized itineraries." This mission highlights your dedication to creating luxurious, tailored experiences and emphasizes customer satisfaction as a top priority.

Your mission and vision should be more than just words on paper. They should guide every decision you make, from the type of trips you offer to the way you interact with clients. If your vision is to promote sustainable tourism, then every aspect of your business—from choosing eco-friendly suppliers to educating clients about their environmental impact—should reflect that commitment.

Your vision and mission will also play a crucial role in shaping your brand identity. They communicate to potential clients what your agency stands for and what they can expect from working with you. As you grow, your vision and mission will help you stay focused and aligned with your long-term goals, especially during challenging times or as the industry evolves.

In summary, defining your vision and niche is essential to establishing a travel agency that stands out in a competitive market. By understanding the various segments of the travel industry, choosing a focused niche, and setting a clear vision and mission, you can build a strong foundation for your business. Your niche will allow you to target a specific audience, while your vision and mission will guide your growth and ensure that you remain true to your core values as your agency expands.

Chapter 2:
Market Research and Feasibility Study

When launching a travel agency, one of the most critical steps in your journey is conducting thorough market research and a feasibility study. These processes will provide you with invaluable insights into your potential customers, competitors, and the broader travel industry landscape. Understanding these elements will allow you to position your business strategically, tailor your services to specific needs, and determine whether your business idea is viable in the current market.

Identifying Target Markets

To build a successful travel agency, you must first identify your target market. Understanding your potential customers is the foundation of your business. Who are they? What drives their travel decisions? What do they value most when planning a trip, and what are their primary concerns? The process of identifying your target market involves analyzing key demographics, travel preferences, purchasing behavior, and psychographics.

Demographics include factors such as age, income, education level, occupation, family size, and geographic location. For example, if you specialize in luxury travel, your target audience may consist of affluent professionals, retirees, or families with disposable income who seek high-end, exclusive experiences. Conversely, if your focus is budget-friendly travel, your target market may be younger travelers, students, or families looking for affordable vacation options.

Age is a particularly important demographic in the travel industry. Millennials and Gen Z travelers, for instance, often prioritize unique, immersive experiences and are more likely to book trips based on social media inspiration. They are also more likely to book trips online and seek out independent, adventurous travel. On the other hand, baby boomers and older generations may prioritize comfort, safety, and convenience, with a preference for pre-arranged tours, cruises, or luxury stays.

Another key factor is income and spending habits. Travelers' budgets will influence their preferences for destinations, accommodations, and activities. Those with higher incomes may opt for five-star hotels, private tours, or first-class airfare, while budget-conscious travelers might prioritize finding deals on flights, choosing economy lodging, and seeking affordable travel experiences.

Next, you'll need to assess the travel preferences of your target market. Some customers may prefer adventure travel, such as hiking, trekking, or exploring remote regions, while others may be interested in cultural tourism, luxury vacations, or family-friendly trips. Business travelers, on the other hand, will have different needs, such as efficient booking processes, access to conference facilities, and comfortable accommodations for short stays. Understanding these preferences will help you design travel packages and services that meet their specific needs.

In addition to demographics and preferences, it's also essential to consider psychographic factors. Psychographics delve deeper into the attitudes, interests, and lifestyle choices of your potential customers. For example, some travelers may be motivated by a desire for sustainability and eco-friendly travel options, while others may prioritize relaxation, personal growth, or adventure. By understanding the motivations behind your customers' travel decisions, you can better tailor your offerings to align with their values.

Another critical aspect of identifying your target market is recognizing the pain points and challenges that travelers face. For instance, solo travelers may be concerned about safety and security, especially when traveling to unfamiliar destinations. Families might prioritize kid-friendly accommodations and activities, while business travelers may value convenience and time-saving services. By understanding these pain points, you can position your agency as a solution to your customers' challenges, offering personalized services that alleviate their concerns.

Finally, consider conducting surveys, focus groups, or interviews with potential customers to gather direct feedback about their travel preferences, habits, and unmet needs. This primary research can provide you with real-world data that will inform your business strategy and help you refine your target audience.

Identifying your target market is not a one-time task. As the travel industry evolves and consumer preferences shift, it's essential to stay attuned to these changes. By continually analyzing your target audience and adapting your services to meet their needs, you can ensure that your travel agency remains relevant and competitive in the market.

Analyzing Competitors

Once you have a clear understanding of your target market, the next step is to analyze your competitors. A competitive analysis will help you identify the strengths and weaknesses of other travel agencies operating in your niche and give you insights into how to position your business effectively.

The first step in this process is to identify your direct competitors. These are agencies that offer similar services to your target market. For example, if you plan to specialize in eco-friendly adventure travel, your competitors may include other adventure travel companies, sustainable tourism operators, or online booking platforms that cater to eco-conscious travelers. You should also consider indirect competitors, such as larger online travel agencies (OTAs) like Expedia or Booking.com, which may not specialize in your niche but still compete for the same customers.

Start by researching your competitors' offerings. What types of travel packages do they provide? Are they focused on budget-friendly vacations, luxury experiences, corporate travel, or adventure tourism? Do they offer customizable itineraries, guided tours, or all-inclusive packages? By understanding what your competitors are offering, you can identify opportunities to differentiate your business.

Next, evaluate your competitors' pricing strategies. How do they price their services, and what value do they offer for the price? Pricing is a critical factor in the travel industry, and understanding the pricing landscape will help you determine whether you want to position your agency as a premium service provider or a more affordable option. You may also discover pricing gaps in the market that you can exploit, such as offering mid-range packages for travelers who are looking for a balance between cost and experience.

In addition to their offerings and pricing, you should assess your competitors' marketing strategies. How do they promote their services? What channels do they use to reach their audience? Are they leveraging social media, influencer partnerships, email marketing, or search engine optimization (SEO) to attract customers? By studying your competitors' marketing efforts, you can identify successful tactics that you may want to replicate or gaps that you can fill with your own marketing strategy.

Another important aspect of competitor analysis is assessing the customer experience. This includes everything from how easy it is to navigate their website and book a trip to the level of customer service they provide throughout the travel process. You can gather this information by reading customer reviews, visiting competitor websites, and even booking a trip yourself to experience their service firsthand. Look for areas where your competitors excel and where they fall short. For example, if customers frequently complain about poor communication or unclear cancellation policies, you can ensure that your agency provides better service in these areas.

Pay attention to your competitors' brand positioning as well. How do they present themselves to their audience? Are they promoting themselves as experts in luxury travel, adventure tourism, or budget vacations? What is their unique selling proposition (USP), and how do they differentiate themselves from other agencies? Understanding how your competitors position their brands will help you craft your own brand identity and value proposition.

As part of your competitor analysis, also consider the technological tools and platforms your competitors are using. Many travel agencies now rely on online booking systems, mobile apps, virtual tours, and AI-powered chatbots to enhance the customer experience. By analyzing the technology used by your competitors, you can identify opportunities to leverage similar or more advanced tools to streamline your own operations and improve customer satisfaction.

Competitor analysis is an ongoing process. The travel industry is constantly changing, with new players entering the market and existing competitors evolving their services. Regularly revisiting your competitive landscape will allow you to stay ahead of trends, identify new opportunities, and continually refine your business strategy.

Assessing Industry Trends

The travel industry is heavily influenced by global events, technological advancements, and changing consumer preferences. To build a successful and sustainable travel agency, it's crucial to stay informed about the latest industry trends and adapt your business to meet the evolving needs of travelers.

One of the most significant trends in recent years is the rise of digital nomadism. The COVID-19 pandemic accelerated the adoption of remote work, allowing more people to work from anywhere in the world. Digital nomads are individuals who combine work and travel, often staying in a destination for an extended period. As a result, there is a growing demand for travel services that cater to this demographic, such as long-term accommodation options, co-working spaces, and visa assistance. Travel agencies that specialize in digital nomad services can create customized packages that provide both work-friendly environments and exciting travel experiences.

Another trend gaining momentum is solo travel. More and more travelers, especially women, are embarking on solo journeys to explore new destinations on their own terms. This trend presents an opportunity for travel agencies to offer specialized services for solo travelers, such as personalized itineraries, small-group tours, and safety-focused travel advice. Agencies can also create packages that cater to specific interests, such as wellness retreats, cultural immersion, or adventure sports, to appeal to solo travelers seeking unique experiences.

Eco-friendly and sustainable tourism is another major trend shaping the travel industry. As environmental awareness grows, travelers are increasingly seeking out destinations and experiences that minimize their environmental impact. Sustainable tourism focuses on reducing carbon footprints, supporting local communities, and preserving natural and cultural heritage. Travel agencies that prioritize sustainability can differentiate themselves by offering eco-friendly accommodations, promoting responsible wildlife tourism, and partnering with local businesses that practice sustainable tourism. Incorporating sustainability into your business model can also attract environmentally conscious travelers who value ethical and responsible travel.

Health and wellness tourism is a rapidly growing niche within the travel industry. In a world where stress and burnout are common, many travelers are seeking trips that focus on relaxation, rejuvenation, and personal well-being. Wellness tourism includes experiences such as spa retreats, yoga and meditation retreats, detox programs, and fitness holidays. By offering health and wellness travel packages, your agency can tap into this growing market of travelers looking to improve their mental and physical health while exploring new destinations.

Cultural and immersive experiences have also become increasingly popular among travelers. Today's travelers want more than just sightseeing; they want to connect with local cultures, traditions, and people. This has led to a surge in demand for cultural tours, cooking classes, homestays, and volunteer tourism. Travel agencies that can offer authentic, immersive experiences will appeal to travelers seeking meaningful connections and unique cultural insights.

Another trend to watch is the rise of technological advancements in the travel industry. From artificial intelligence (AI) and virtual reality (VR) to blockchain and contactless payments, technology is reshaping the way people travel. Virtual tours, for example, allow travelers to explore destinations remotely before booking a trip, while AI-powered chatbots provide instant customer support. As a travel agency, staying up-to-date with the latest technological innovations can help you streamline operations, enhance the customer experience, and stay competitive in the market.

The travel industry is also heavily influenced by global events. The COVID-19 pandemic had a profound impact on the industry, leading to travel restrictions, changing consumer behavior, and a greater focus on health and safety. While the industry is recovering, it's essential to stay prepared for potential future disruptions. Travelers may prioritize flexibility in booking policies, safety protocols, and travel insurance in the years to come. Agencies that can offer peace of mind through clear communication, flexible policies, and health-conscious travel options will be well-positioned to attract cautious travelers.

Lastly, consider the growing importance of personalization in travel. Today's travelers expect tailored experiences that match their preferences, from customized itineraries to personalized recommendations. Leveraging data and customer insights can help your agency offer more personalized services, whether it's suggesting destinations based on past trips or offering travel packages that cater to specific interests. Personalization can create a more memorable and satisfying travel experience, leading to higher customer retention and loyalty.

By staying informed about industry trends, you can position your travel agency to capitalize on emerging opportunities and remain competitive in a rapidly evolving market. Regularly monitoring trends and adapting your business strategy will ensure that your agency stays relevant and continues to meet the changing needs of travelers.

Conclusion: The Importance of Market Research and Feasibility Studies

Conducting market research and a feasibility study is essential to the success of your travel agency. By identifying your target markets, analyzing competitors, and staying informed about industry trends, you can build a solid foundation for your business. These processes will help you refine your business model, differentiate your services, and ensure that your agency is well-positioned to meet the needs of your customers.

In addition, a feasibility study will help you assess the practicality and profitability of your business idea. It will provide you with a clear understanding of the market demand for your services, the financial investment required to start and sustain your business, and the potential challenges you may face. This analysis will allow you to make informed decisions and reduce the risk of failure.

Ultimately, the key to success in the travel industry lies in your ability to adapt to change. The travel landscape is constantly evolving, influenced by technological advancements, global events, and shifting consumer preferences. By conducting regular market research and staying attuned to industry trends, you can ensure that your travel agency remains relevant, competitive, and prepared to thrive in the ever-changing world of travel.

Chapter 3:
Creating a Business Plan

Creating a business plan is one of the most crucial steps in building a successful travel agency. A well-crafted business plan serves as a roadmap, guiding you through the process of setting up and growing your business. It forces you to think through every aspect of your venture, from marketing and operations to financial projections and risk management. This chapter will take a deep dive into every component of a solid business plan, ensuring that you're thoroughly prepared for the road ahead.

Executive Summary

The Executive Summary is arguably the most important part of your business plan because it provides a high-level overview of your travel agency and summarizes the key points that will be detailed in the rest of the document. Although it's typically the first section in a business plan, many entrepreneurs find it easier to write the Executive Summary last, after they've worked through the finer details of the other sections.

The Executive Summary should capture the essence of your travel agency—its mission, target market, unique selling proposition (USP), and how it plans to operate. It should clearly state your business goals and provide a snapshot of the financial projections. This section is meant to grab the reader's attention and compel them to keep reading, whether they are potential investors, partners, or other stakeholders. As a rule of thumb, keep the Executive Summary concise—no more than two pages—yet comprehensive enough to give a full picture of what your travel agency is about.

Start by introducing your travel agency and your vision for the business. Explain why you decided to start a travel agency, what gap in the market you're filling, and how you plan to provide value to your customers. This should be followed by a brief explanation of your target market and how your agency is uniquely positioned to meet their needs. Highlight your unique selling proposition (USP) and any competitive advantages your business has.

Next, outline the basic financials, such as projected revenue, startup costs, and profitability. You don't need to go into extreme detail here—that will be covered in the financial section—but you should provide an overview that gives readers a sense of the financial viability of your travel agency.

Finally, wrap up the Executive Summary with a summary of your business goals, both short-term and long-term. Include any milestones you plan to hit in the first few years, such as expanding your customer base, launching new services, or achieving profitability.

Company Description

The Company Description provides a more detailed explanation of what your travel agency is and the market it serves. This section goes beyond the brief introduction in the Executive Summary to paint a comprehensive picture of your business.

Start by explaining your company's mission and vision. The mission statement should succinctly capture the purpose of your travel agency and how it intends to serve its customers. For example, your mission might be to "provide customized, unforgettable travel experiences that immerse travelers in the local culture, all while promoting sustainable tourism." The vision statement should be forward-looking and describe where you see the company in the future, such as becoming a leading provider of eco-friendly travel packages or expanding your services to multiple international markets.

Next, describe the type of travel agency you plan to operate. Will you focus on luxury travel, adventure tourism, corporate travel, or another niche? Perhaps you want to specialize in family-friendly vacations, honeymoons, or group tours. Being clear about your niche is essential because it will inform the rest of your business plan, from marketing to service offerings.

The legal structure of your business should also be mentioned here. Are you operating as a sole proprietorship, partnership, limited liability company (LLC), or corporation? Each of these structures has different implications for how your business is taxed, your level of personal liability, and your administrative responsibilities. If you're unsure of which structure to choose, it's wise to consult with an attorney or accountant to help you decide.

You should also include information about the ownership of your travel agency. If there are multiple owners or partners, describe who they are, what their roles in the company will be, and how ownership is divided. If you're the sole owner, this section will be brief but should still explain your role in the company and any relevant experience you bring to the table.

Finally, provide some background on the industry and market in which your travel agency will operate. This is your opportunity to demonstrate your understanding of the travel industry and how your business will fit into the larger market. Discuss trends in the industry, such as the rise of eco-tourism, the impact of technology on travel planning, or changes in consumer preferences. Highlight any opportunities you see in the market and explain how your travel agency is uniquely positioned to capitalize on them.

Market Research and Target Audience
Understanding your target market is crucial for the success of your travel agency. Without a clear understanding of who your

customers are and what they want, it will be difficult to effectively market your services or provide experiences that truly resonate with your audience. In this section of your business plan, you will outline the research you've conducted to identify your target market and provide a detailed description of your ideal customers.

Start by identifying the demographics of your target audience. This includes basic information such as age, gender, income level, occupation, education, and geographic location. Depending on your niche, you might be targeting millennials seeking adventure travel, families looking for kid-friendly vacation packages, or retirees interested in luxury cruises. Be as specific as possible when describing your ideal customers, as this will help you tailor your services and marketing efforts to their needs.

Next, delve into the psychographics of your target audience. Psychographics go beyond demographics to explore the attitudes, interests, and motivations of your customers. What drives them to travel? Are they seeking relaxation, adventure, cultural immersion, or personal growth? Are they motivated by a desire for eco-friendly travel options, or are they primarily concerned with finding the best deals? Understanding the underlying motivations of your customers will allow you to create more compelling marketing messages and design travel experiences that truly resonate with them.

You should also analyze the buying behavior of your target audience. How do they typically book travel? Do they prefer to book online, through a travel agent, or directly with hotels and airlines? What factors influence their purchasing decisions, such as price, convenience, or the level of personalization offered? By understanding how your customers make decisions, you can design your services to meet their needs and preferences.

After outlining the demographics, psychographics, and buying behavior of your target audience, provide an overview of the market size and growth potential for your niche. How large is the market for the type of travel you plan to offer? Is it growing, stable, or declining? If possible, provide statistics and data to support your analysis. For example, if you're targeting adventure travelers, you might cite research showing that the adventure travel market is expected to grow by a certain percentage over the next five years.

Finally, consider any challenges or barriers to entry you might face when targeting your market. For example, if you're entering a highly competitive market, it might be difficult to differentiate your services from those of established competitors. Alternatively, if you're targeting a niche market that is underserved, you might face challenges in educating potential customers about the benefits of your services. By identifying these challenges upfront, you can develop strategies to overcome them and position your business for success.

Competitive Analysis

Understanding your competition is just as important as understanding your target market. In this section, you'll analyze your competitors to identify their strengths and weaknesses, assess their market positioning, and determine how your travel agency can differentiate itself.

Start by identifying your direct competitors—other travel agencies that offer similar services to your target market. For example, if you plan to specialize in eco-friendly travel, your direct competitors might include other agencies that offer sustainable travel packages. You should also consider your indirect competitors, such as online travel agencies (OTAs) like Expedia or Booking.com, which may not specialize in your niche but still compete for the same customers.

Once you've identified your competitors, analyze their service offerings. What types of travel packages do they offer? Are they focused on budget travel, luxury experiences, or a specific type of vacation, such as cruises or guided tours? Understanding the range of services your competitors provide will help you identify any gaps in the market that your agency can fill. For example, if none of your competitors offer personalized, eco-friendly travel experiences, this could be an opportunity for your business.

Next, assess your competitors' pricing strategies. How do they price their services, and what value do they offer for the price? Are they competing primarily on price, or do they differentiate themselves based on the quality of their services or the unique experiences they offer? Understanding the pricing landscape in your market will help you determine how to position your own services and whether you want to compete on price, quality, or both.

In addition to service offerings and pricing, evaluate your competitors' marketing strategies. How do they reach their customers? Are they using social media, email marketing, search engine optimization (SEO), or other channels to promote their services? What messaging do they use in their marketing campaigns, and how do they position themselves in the market? By analyzing your competitors' marketing efforts, you can identify successful tactics that you might want to replicate, as well as areas where you can differentiate your agency.

Another important aspect of competitive analysis is assessing the customer experience. How easy is it to book a trip with your competitors? Do they offer a user-friendly website, responsive customer service, and clear cancellation policies? Are there any common complaints in customer reviews, such as poor communication or unexpected fees? By understanding how your competitors interact with their customers, you can identify opportunities to improve the customer experience at your own agency.

Finally, consider your competitors' brand positioning. How do they present themselves in the market? Are they seen as a budget-friendly option, a luxury provider, or a niche specialist? Understanding how your competitors position their brands will help you define your own brand and ensure that it stands out in the market.

By conducting a thorough competitive analysis, you'll gain valuable insights into the strengths and weaknesses of your competitors. This information will help you identify opportunities to differentiate your travel agency, refine your service offerings, and develop a unique value proposition that sets you apart from the competition.

Marketing and Sales Strategy

A well-defined marketing and sales strategy is essential for attracting customers and growing your travel agency. In this section, you'll outline the strategies you'll use to promote your business, reach your target audience, and convert leads into sales.

Start by defining your marketing objectives. What do you hope to achieve with your marketing efforts? For example, your goals might include increasing brand awareness, generating leads, building a loyal customer base, or establishing your agency as a trusted authority in a specific niche. Be specific and set measurable goals, such as achieving a certain number of website visitors, social media followers, or bookings within a set timeframe.

Next, outline the marketing channels you'll use to promote your travel agency. There are numerous marketing channels to choose from, and the best ones for your business will depend on your target audience and marketing objectives. Some common channels for travel agencies include:

Social Media Marketing: Platforms like Instagram, Facebook, and Pinterest are particularly effective for promoting travel experiences, as they allow you to showcase visually appealing destinations and engage with potential customers. Use these platforms to share photos and videos of the trips you offer, promote special deals, and interact with your audience.

Search Engine Optimization (SEO): SEO is the process of optimizing your website so that it ranks higher in search engine results pages (SERPs). By targeting relevant keywords, such as "adventure travel packages" or "luxury cruises," you can attract organic traffic from people searching for the types of trips you offer.

Content Marketing: Creating high-quality content, such as blog posts, travel guides, and videos, can help establish your travel agency as an authority in your niche. For example, you might create a blog post titled "Top 10 Eco-Friendly Travel Destinations" or a video that showcases a recent group tour you organized.

Email Marketing: Building an email list of potential customers allows you to nurture leads over time and keep your audience informed about special offers, new travel packages, or travel tips. Sending personalized emails based on customer preferences can also help increase engagement and conversion rates.

Pay-Per-Click (PPC) Advertising: PPC ads, such as Google Ads or Facebook Ads, allow you to target specific audiences with your marketing messages. You only pay when someone clicks on your ad, making it a cost-effective way to drive traffic to your website and generate leads.

Referral Programs: Encouraging satisfied customers to refer friends and family to your agency can be a powerful way to generate new business. Offer incentives, such as discounts or travel vouchers, for successful referrals.

Once you've outlined your marketing channels, describe the messaging and branding you'll use in your campaigns. What message do you want to convey to potential customers, and how will your branding reflect the values and experiences your agency offers? For example, if you're focused on eco-friendly travel, your messaging might emphasize sustainability, adventure, and connection with nature. Be consistent in your messaging across all marketing channels to build a strong, recognizable brand.

In addition to your marketing strategy, you'll need a clear sales strategy to convert leads into customers. This might involve setting up a user-friendly booking system on your website, providing personalized travel consultations, or offering flexible payment options. Consider the sales process from the customer's perspective and identify any barriers that might prevent them from booking a trip. For example, if customers are unsure about the value of your services, offering testimonials, reviews, or case studies can help build trust and confidence.

Finally, outline how you'll measure the success of your marketing and sales efforts. What key performance indicators (KPIs) will you track to determine whether your strategies are working? Common KPIs for travel agencies include website traffic, conversion rates, social media engagement, and customer satisfaction. By regularly reviewing your KPIs, you can identify what's working and make adjustments to improve your marketing and sales performance.

Service Offerings and Operations Plan

In this section, you'll outline the specific services your travel agency will offer and how you'll operate your business on a day-to-day basis. This is where you'll go into detail about the types of travel packages you'll provide, how you'll fulfill customer requests, and the logistics of running your agency.

Start by describing your service offerings. Will you offer pre-packaged trips, customized itineraries, or a combination of both? What types of trips will you specialize in, such as luxury vacations, adventure tours, or corporate travel? Be specific about the services you'll provide, such as booking flights and accommodations, arranging transportation, organizing guided tours, or offering travel insurance.

If you plan to offer customized travel experiences, explain how the process will work. For example, will customers be able to request personalized itineraries based on their preferences, such as specific destinations, activities, or accommodations? How will you ensure that each customer receives a unique and tailored experience? Providing personalized services can be a key differentiator for your travel agency, but it also requires a clear process for gathering customer information, planning the itinerary, and managing logistics.

Next, outline the vendors and partnerships you'll rely on to fulfill customer requests. Travel agencies typically work with a network of suppliers, such as airlines, hotels, tour operators, and transportation companies, to provide services to their customers. Identify the vendors you'll partner with and explain how you'll manage these relationships. For example, will you work with specific hotel chains or tour operators to offer exclusive deals? How will you ensure that your vendors provide high-quality services that meet your customers' expectations?

The operations plan should also cover the day-to-day logistics of running your travel agency. This includes everything from managing bookings and customer inquiries to handling payments and cancellations. If you plan to operate an online travel agency, describe the technology and software you'll use to manage bookings, process payments, and communicate with customers. For example, will you use a customer relationship management (CRM) system to track customer interactions and manage leads? Will you integrate a booking platform with your website to streamline the reservation process?

If you plan to operate a brick-and-mortar travel agency, explain the layout and location of your physical office. Will you have a storefront where customers can walk in and book trips, or will you operate out of a home office and conduct business primarily online or over the phone? Be sure to describe any equipment, software, or personnel you'll need to run the day-to-day operations smoothly.

Finally, include a plan for customer service. Excellent customer service is essential for building a loyal customer base and generating repeat business. How will you handle customer inquiries, complaints, and issues that arise before, during, or after a trip? Will you offer 24/7 customer support, or will you have set business hours? Consider offering multiple channels for customers to reach you, such as phone, email, and live chat, to provide a seamless experience.

Financial Plan and Projections

The Financial Plan and Projections section is where you'll outline the financial aspects of your travel agency, including startup costs, revenue streams, and profitability projections. This section is crucial for demonstrating the financial viability of your business and attracting potential investors or lenders.

Start by outlining your startup costs. This includes any expenses you'll incur before your travel agency is operational, such as business registration fees, website development, marketing materials, and office equipment. Be as detailed as possible in listing these expenses, as underestimating startup costs can lead to cash flow problems down the line.

Next, identify your revenue streams. How will your travel agency generate income? Will you earn commissions from booking flights, hotels, and tours? Will you charge customers a fee for customized itineraries or premium services? Consider all potential sources of revenue, including upselling travel insurance, offering group discounts, or selling additional services like airport transfers.

Once you've outlined your revenue streams, provide financial projections for the first three to five years of your business. This should include:

Revenue projections: Estimate how much income your travel agency will generate each year, based on factors such as the number of customers you expect to serve, the average booking value, and your commission rates. Be realistic in your projections and base them on thorough market research and competitor analysis.

Expense projections: Estimate your ongoing expenses, including salaries, office rent, marketing costs, and software subscriptions. Be sure to include any variable costs, such as commissions paid to vendors or transportation costs for organizing tours.

Profit and loss statements: Create a projected profit and loss (P&L) statement that shows your expected revenue, expenses, and profits for each year. This will give you a clear picture of your business's financial health and help you determine when you'll break even or achieve profitability.

Cash flow projections: Cash flow is crucial for the survival of any business, especially in the early stages. Create a cash flow projection that outlines when you expect money to come in and go out of your business. This will help you identify any potential cash flow gaps and plan for how to manage them.

Break-even analysis: A break-even analysis will help you determine how much revenue your travel agency needs to generate in order to cover its costs. This is an important metric for understanding the financial viability of your business and setting realistic revenue goals.

Finally, consider any funding requirements you may have. Will you need to secure loans or investments to cover your startup costs or fund your initial marketing efforts? If so, outline how much funding you'll need and how you plan to use it. Be prepared to present this information to potential investors or lenders in a clear and compelling way.

Risk Management and Contingency Plan

Every business faces risks, and a successful travel agency is no exception. In this section, you'll outline the risks your business might face and how you plan to mitigate them. This is an important part of your business plan, as it demonstrates that you've thought through potential challenges and have a plan in place to handle them.

Start by identifying the key risks associated with running a travel agency. These might include:

Market risks: Changes in consumer preferences, economic downturns, or increased competition can impact your business's ability to attract and retain customers.

Operational risks: This includes risks related to the day-to-day operations of your agency, such as software failures, supplier issues, or employee turnover.

Financial risks: Cash flow problems, unexpected expenses, or difficulties in securing funding can put your business at risk.

Legal and regulatory risks: Travel agencies must comply with various laws and regulations, such as consumer protection laws, data privacy regulations, and travel industry standards. Failing to comply with these regulations can result in fines or legal disputes.

External risks: External factors such as natural disasters, pandemics, or geopolitical instability can disrupt travel plans and negatively impact your business.

For each risk, outline a mitigation strategy. What steps will you take to minimize the likelihood or impact of these risks? For example, you might reduce market risk by diversifying your service offerings or targeting multiple customer segments. You could mitigate operational risk by investing in reliable software and building strong relationships with trusted suppliers.

In addition to your risk mitigation strategies, develop a contingency plan for dealing with unexpected events. What will you do if a major supplier goes out of business, or if there's a sudden drop in demand for travel services? Having a contingency plan in place will help you respond quickly and effectively to unforeseen challenges, minimizing the impact on your business.

Finally, consider whether you need insurance to protect your business from certain risks. Common types of insurance for travel agencies include professional liability insurance, which covers legal costs in case a customer sues you for negligence, and business interruption insurance, which covers lost income if your business is disrupted by an unforeseen event.

Creating a business plan is a critical step in launching a successful travel agency. It serves as a roadmap for your business, guiding your decisions and helping you stay focused on your goals. A well-thought-out business plan can also be a valuable tool for attracting investors or securing loans, as it demonstrates that you've carefully considered all aspects of your business and have a clear strategy for achieving success.

By following the steps outlined in this chapter, you'll be well on your way to creating a comprehensive business plan that sets your travel agency up for success. Whether you're just starting out or looking to grow your existing business, a solid business plan will help you navigate the challenges and opportunities of the travel industry with confidence.

Chapter 4:
Legal Requirements and Certifications

Starting a travel agency can be an exciting and profitable venture, but it also comes with a host of legal requirements and industry certifications that are essential for the operation of your business. Understanding and navigating these legal frameworks is crucial to ensuring that your travel agency is both compliant and well-protected. In this chapter, we will explore the various legal requirements you need to fulfill, from licensing and registration to obtaining the necessary certifications. We'll also discuss the importance of travel insurance and liability coverage to protect your business from potential risks. By the end of this chapter, you'll have a clear understanding of the steps you need to take to legally operate your travel agency and establish yourself as a trusted professional in the industry.

Licensing and Registration

One of the first and most crucial steps in starting your travel agency is ensuring that you meet all the licensing and registration requirements necessary to legally operate. These requirements can vary significantly depending on your location, so it's critical to do thorough research based on where your business will be headquartered. Navigating the legal landscape of the travel industry may seem daunting, but understanding these essentials will lay a solid foundation for your agency's success.

Researching Legal Requirements by Location
Each country, and in some cases, individual states or provinces within countries, has different laws governing the operation of travel agencies. In the United States, for example, certain states impose more stringent licensing requirements than others. States like California, Florida, and Hawaii have specific seller of travel laws that govern how travel agencies must operate within their jurisdictions. These laws often require travel agencies to register

with the state, obtain a seller of travel license, and sometimes even post a bond as a form of financial protection for customers. This bond is essentially an insurance policy that protects consumers if the travel agency fails to provide the services paid for or goes bankrupt.

In Canada, travel agents must be licensed by their province, with requirements varying between provinces like Ontario, British Columbia, and Quebec. Each province has its own regulatory framework that governs travel agency operations, often focusing on consumer protection and ethical business practices. For example, Ontario requires travel agencies to have a license that is renewed periodically, while British Columbia mandates registration with Consumer Protection BC. Understanding these provincial laws is essential for compliance and to ensure that your agency operates legally and ethically.

Meanwhile, in countries like the United Kingdom and Australia, travel agents are required to follow a different set of regulations that focus on ensuring consumer protection. For instance, travel agencies in the UK often belong to organizations such as the Association of British Travel Agents (ABTA), which enforces strict codes of conduct and provides consumer protection schemes. Compliance with these regulations not only enhances your agency's credibility but also helps you avoid potential legal pitfalls.

It's also crucial to consider if you're planning to offer specialized travel services, such as cruise vacations or international travel packages, as these may require additional licenses or certifications. For example, agencies that specialize in cruise travel might need to adhere to maritime regulations and have specific insurance policies. Similarly, offering international travel may necessitate compliance with various country-specific laws that govern travel services, ensuring that you are adequately protected and compliant with local regulations. Researching the specific requirements for the types of services you plan to offer will help ensure you're compliant with all applicable laws.

Registering Your Business

In addition to obtaining the appropriate travel agency licenses, you'll also need to register your business with the relevant government authorities. This process is essential for legally operating within your jurisdiction and involves several key steps. In many countries, this involves registering your business with local, state, or national tax authorities. You may need to apply for a business license from your local government, which allows you to legally operate within your city or municipality.

Next, you'll likely need to register for a tax identification number (TIN) or employer identification number (EIN), which is crucial for filing business taxes, hiring employees, and opening business bank accounts. This identification number is essential for the legal and financial operation of your agency, as it separates your personal finances from your business finances. In most jurisdictions, you are also required to pay sales tax on the services you sell, so you'll need to register for a sales tax permit. This will ensure that you collect and remit sales tax appropriately, which is an important aspect of running a legitimate business.

The process of business registration is typically straightforward but can vary depending on your location and the structure of your business. Whether you choose to operate as a sole proprietor, limited liability company (LLC), or corporation, understanding the pros and cons of each business structure is essential. An LLC, for example, offers the benefit of limited personal liability, protecting your personal assets in the event of business debts or legal issues. A corporation may provide more opportunities for investment and growth, allowing you to bring in partners or investors as your business expands. Carefully evaluating these structures will help you choose the one that best aligns with your business goals and risk tolerance.

International Considerations
If you're planning to operate an international travel agency, you'll also need to consider the cross-border legal requirements. Many countries require travel agencies that arrange international travel to comply with their regulations, which can include applying for special permits, registering as a foreign business, and adhering to the tax laws of those countries. For example, agencies booking European travel packages may need to adhere to the EU Package Travel Directive, which outlines consumer protection requirements for travel bookings within the European Union. This directive includes essential provisions such as the right to clear information, the right to change or cancel bookings, and the protection of customers' payments in the event of supplier bankruptcy.

In addition to understanding international laws, you'll need to keep abreast of the ever-changing geopolitical landscape that can affect travel, such as visa requirements, travel advisories, and other regulations that may influence how you operate your agency. It's vital to develop a comprehensive understanding of these international considerations, as they can have a significant impact on your agency's operations and the services you offer.

Consumer Protection Laws
Another key aspect of legal compliance is adhering to consumer protection laws. Many countries have strict consumer protection regulations that apply to travel agencies, ensuring that customers receive accurate information, fair prices, and the services they pay for. In the United States, for instance, the Truth in Travel Advertising Act prohibits travel agencies from making false or misleading statements in their marketing materials. This legislation

mandates that all advertising must be truthful and not deceptive, which helps protect consumers from fraudulent practices.

Similarly, the U.S. Department of Transportation regulates the advertising and sale of airfares, ensuring that travel agencies display accurate pricing information and disclose any additional fees that may apply. Transparency is critical in building trust with your clients, and adherence to these regulations helps maintain that trust.

In the European Union, travel agencies must comply with the Package Travel and Linked Travel Arrangements Directive, which provides a high level of protection for consumers who book travel packages. This includes requirements around providing clear information about services, offering refunds in the case of cancellations, and ensuring that customers are protected if a travel provider goes bankrupt. Compliance with these laws not only protects consumers but also reinforces your agency's commitment to ethical business practices.

By thoroughly researching the legal requirements for operating a travel agency in your location, registering your business, and adhering to consumer protection laws, you'll ensure that your agency is compliant and can avoid potential legal complications down the line. This diligence in establishing a solid legal foundation will enable you to focus on what truly matters: providing exceptional travel experiences for your clients while building a reputable and successful agency.

Obtaining Industry Certifications

In addition to meeting the legal requirements to operate a travel agency, obtaining industry certifications can be a valuable way to establish your credibility and gain access to important resources. Certifications from recognized organizations such as the

International Air Transport Association (IATA) and the American Society of Travel Advisors (ASTA) can significantly bolster your professional reputation while providing tools and networks that facilitate the effective operation of your agency.

International Air Transport Association (IATA) Certification
One of the most prestigious certifications available to travel agencies is the IATA certification. The International Air Transport Association represents airlines globally and plays a pivotal role in the regulation of air travel and ticket sales. IATA certification is widely recognized as a hallmark of excellence in the travel industry, granting agencies access to a variety of resources and benefits essential for operations.

With IATA certification, your agency can participate in the Billing and Settlement Plan (BSP), which streamlines the processes of booking and payment for airline tickets. The BSP serves as a central clearinghouse for ticket sales, allowing agencies to manage payments efficiently and receive commissions more reliably. Additionally, IATA certification empowers agencies to issue Airline Reporting Corporation (ARC) tickets, a necessity for booking flights with many leading airlines.

To achieve IATA certification, your travel agency must meet specific eligibility criteria, including demonstrating financial stability, maintaining a professional office environment, and possessing the appropriate licenses. The application process generally requires submitting financial documents, proof of insurance, and detailed information about your agency's operations. Once certified, your agency will be assigned an IATA number, which uniquely identifies your business within the industry and facilitates access to various booking platforms.

American Society of Travel Advisors (ASTA) Membership

Another valuable certification is membership with the American Society of Travel Advisors (ASTA), a leading professional organization for travel agents in the United States. ASTA provides a wealth of resources, including the latest industry news, educational opportunities, and networking events. Joining ASTA enables you to stay updated on industry trends, access exclusive training programs, and connect with fellow travel professionals.

ASTA also offers certifications like the Verified Travel Advisor (VTA) designation, which signifies your expertise and dedication to delivering exceptional client service. To earn the VTA certification, agents must complete a series of courses covering essential topics such as ethics, legal compliance, and business management. Achieving the VTA certification can help distinguish your agency from competitors and reassure clients that they are engaging with a knowledgeable and committed professional.

Beyond educational resources, ASTA actively advocates for travel agents at both state and federal levels, lobbying for policies that benefit the travel industry and protect consumers. By joining ASTA, you not only enhance your agency's professional credibility but also contribute to the broader support network for travel agents.

Other Industry Certifications
In addition to IATA and ASTA, various other certifications and associations can benefit travel agents based on their specific service offerings. For example, if you focus on cruise travel, consider joining the Cruise Lines International Association (CLIA), which provides training programs and certifications for cruise specialists. CLIA certification can enhance your knowledge of the cruise industry, allowing you to offer informed advice and tailored packages to clients.

If luxury travel is your niche, certifications such as the Certified Travel Counselor (CTC) or Certified Travel Associate (CTA) from The Travel Institute can validate your expertise in providing high-end travel services. These certifications equip you with the knowledge and skills necessary to meet the unique needs of luxury travelers.

Pursuing these certifications not only strengthens your agency's credibility but also provides access to essential industry resources, including booking platforms, supplier directories, and ongoing professional development opportunities. By investing in industry certifications, you position yourself to deliver competitive services and grow your travel agency in a dynamic market.

Obtaining industry certifications is a strategic move for any aspiring travel agency owner. It enhances your professional reputation, provides access to critical resources, and equips you with the knowledge needed to navigate the complexities of the travel industry. By committing to these certifications, you not only elevate your agency's standing but also improve your ability to serve clients effectively, ultimately paving the way for long-term success.

Travel Insurance and Liability
As a travel agency, you're responsible for helping clients navigate the complexities of travel, from booking flights and hotels to ensuring their safety and satisfaction throughout their journey. One of the most important aspects of running a travel agency is making sure that both your business and your clients are protected from unexpected events. Travel insurance and liability coverage are essential tools for managing risk and ensuring that your agency is well-prepared to handle any challenges that may arise.

Offering Travel Insurance to Clients

One of the key services you'll provide as a travel agent is offering travel insurance to your clients. Travel insurance helps protect travelers from financial losses due to unexpected events like flight cancellations, medical emergencies, lost luggage, or even natural disasters. By offering travel insurance as part of your service, you're providing clients with peace of mind and ensuring that they're protected from the uncertainties of travel.

There are several types of travel insurance that you can offer, including:

Trip cancellation insurance: This type of insurance reimburses travelers for non-refundable expenses if they need to cancel their trip due to covered reasons, such as illness, injury, or a family emergency.

Medical insurance: Travel medical insurance provides coverage for medical expenses incurred while traveling, including emergency medical treatment, hospitalization, and evacuation. This is particularly important for clients traveling internationally, as their domestic health insurance may not cover them abroad.

Baggage insurance: This type of insurance covers lost, damaged, or stolen luggage, helping travelers recover the cost of their belongings if something goes wrong during their trip.

Travel delay insurance: Travel delay insurance compensates travelers for additional expenses incurred due to flight delays, missed connections, or other travel disruptions.

When offering travel insurance to clients, it's important to partner with a reputable insurance provider that offers comprehensive coverage and excellent customer service. You'll also need to ensure that you're licensed to sell insurance in your state or country, as selling insurance without the proper licensing can result in legal penalties.

Liability Coverage for Your Business
In addition to offering travel insurance to your clients, it's crucial to ensure that your travel agency is protected with the appropriate liability coverage. Liability insurance helps protect your business from legal claims and financial losses that may arise if something goes wrong during the course of your business operations.

There are several types of liability coverage that travel agencies should consider:

Professional liability insurance: Also known as errors and omissions (E&O) insurance, professional liability insurance protects your agency from claims of negligence, mistakes, or failure to deliver promised services. For example, if a client claims that your agency failed to book their hotel correctly, resulting in financial loss, E&O insurance would cover the cost of legal defense and any settlements or judgments against your business.

General liability insurance: General liability insurance protects your agency from claims of bodily injury or property damage that occur on your business premises. For example, if a client slips and falls while visiting your office, general liability insurance would cover the cost of medical expenses and any resulting lawsuits.

Cyber liability insurance: As travel agencies increasingly rely on digital platforms to book travel and store client information, the risk of cyberattacks and data breaches has grown. Cyber liability insurance helps protect your agency from the financial losses associated with data breaches, including the cost of notifying affected clients, legal defense, and potential fines.

By ensuring that your agency has the appropriate liability coverage, you're protecting your business from potential financial ruin in the event of a lawsuit or other legal claim.

Managing Risk and Ensuring Compliance
Travel is inherently unpredictable, and even the most well-planned trips can be disrupted by unforeseen events. From natural disasters to political instability, there are a myriad of risks that can impact your clients' travel experiences. As a travel agent, it's your responsibility to help clients understand these risks and offer solutions to mitigate them.

In addition to offering travel insurance and securing liability coverage, it's important to stay informed about potential risks in the destinations your clients are traveling to. This includes monitoring travel advisories issued by government agencies, staying up-to-date on health and safety concerns, and providing clients with accurate information about any potential hazards they may encounter during their trip.

By taking a proactive approach to risk management, you can help ensure that your clients have a safe and enjoyable travel experience, while also protecting your business from potential legal and financial challenges.

In conclusion, understanding the legal requirements and certifications necessary for running a travel agency is essential to building a successful and sustainable business. By ensuring that you're compliant with local laws, obtaining industry certifications like IATA and ASTA, and offering travel insurance and liability coverage, you'll be well-prepared to navigate the complexities of the travel industry and provide your clients with the best possible service.

Navigating legal frameworks and certifications might seem daunting at first, but these are critical steps toward establishing your credibility, managing risks, and protecting both your clients and your business. By following the guidelines outlined in this chapter, you'll be able to confidently launch and grow your travel agency in a way that's legally compliant, professionally recognized, and well-protected from potential liabilities.

Chapter 5:
Building Partnerships and Supplier Relationships

Building strong partnerships and maintaining excellent supplier relationships are critical to the success of any travel agency. As a travel agent, you're not just a facilitator of trips; you're a bridge between your clients and the various service providers that make their journeys memorable. This chapter focuses on establishing and nurturing those essential partnerships with airlines, hotels, cruise lines, car rental companies, and tour operators, as well as expanding your global network. Additionally, we'll discuss the importance of negotiating commission and compensation models to ensure your business thrives financially.

Working with Travel Suppliers

In the travel industry, one of your primary responsibilities as a travel agent is to establish and maintain strong relationships with a wide range of travel suppliers. These suppliers can include airlines, hotels, cruise lines, car rental companies, and tour operators. By forging strong ties with these entities, you gain access to exclusive deals, special services, and insider information that can make a significant difference in the value you offer your clients. These partnerships also allow you to stand out in a highly competitive market by providing unique experiences and ensuring your clients receive the best possible prices.

Building Relationships with Airlines

Airlines play a pivotal role in the realm of international travel, serving as the essential link between destinations and travelers. Cultivating strong partnerships with airlines is vital for any travel agency aiming to provide clients with the best possible fares and seating options. By developing these relationships, travel agents can gain access to discounted fares and exclusive deals that are not readily available to the general public. Many airlines are willing to offer special pricing or incentives, especially if an agency commits to a certain volume of bookings over a defined period. This mutually beneficial arrangement allows travel agents to deliver value to their clients while ensuring a steady stream of business for the airlines.

Establishing a direct line of communication with airlines or their representatives is crucial for staying informed about the latest promotions, changes in flight schedules, and seat availability. This proactive approach can greatly enhance your agency's ability to respond swiftly to client inquiries and adapt to any shifts in the travel landscape. By being in regular contact with airline representatives, you position your agency to take advantage of new opportunities as they arise, ensuring that you can provide clients with timely information and competitive options.

To initiate and strengthen relationships with airlines, attending industry trade shows and joining travel agent associations can be incredibly beneficial. These events often provide unique opportunities to network directly with airline representatives, allowing you to forge personal connections that can lead to fruitful collaborations. Regular communication and a track record of consistent bookings will help foster trust, demonstrating to the airline that your agency is a reliable partner. Over time, this trust can lead to even better deals and more favorable terms, ultimately benefiting your clients.

Moreover, offering a diverse range of airlines—including both budget and premium options—ensures that you cater to the varied needs and preferences of your clients. Different travelers have different priorities; some may prioritize cost while others may be more focused on comfort or amenities. By providing a spectrum of airline choices, you empower clients to select the travel experience that best fits their requirements, enhancing their overall satisfaction and loyalty to your agency.

Once you've established a strong rapport with an airline, the benefits extend beyond just access to discounted fares. You may also gain access to exclusive amenities such as priority check-in, extra baggage allowances, or seat upgrades for your clients. These added perks can significantly enhance the travel experience, making it more enjoyable and stress-free for your clients. In a competitive market, these differentiators can set your agency apart, positioning you as a preferred choice for travelers seeking both value and exceptional service.

In summary, building strong partnerships with airlines is a fundamental aspect of running a successful travel agency. By securing access to discounted fares, staying informed about industry developments, and providing a range of options to meet diverse client needs, you not only enhance your agency's reputation but also create memorable experiences for your clients. The advantages gained through these relationships—such as exclusive amenities and tailored services—can lead to higher client satisfaction, repeat business, and ultimately, a thriving travel agency.

Partnering with Hotels
Like airlines, hotels are another cornerstone of travel, and the relationships you build with them can directly impact the quality of your clients' experiences. Whether your clients need luxury accommodations, boutique hotels, or budget-friendly lodging, working with a variety of hotels allows you to meet their specific needs.

Establishing relationships with hotel chains and independent hotels can yield special discounts, room upgrades, and exclusive packages. For instance, if you have a client celebrating a honeymoon or anniversary, a good relationship with the hotel might allow you to secure complimentary champagne, a room with a better view, or other perks that can make their stay extraordinary.

Working closely with hotel sales representatives and keeping up-to-date with new developments in the hospitality industry ensures you can provide clients with the latest and greatest options. In return, hotels benefit from your referrals and consistent bookings, which helps to create a mutually beneficial relationship.

Many hotels also offer loyalty programs for travel agents, providing incentives such as free stays, room upgrades, or discounts for personal travel. These programs help build long-term relationships between agents and hotels, and the benefits can be passed on to your clients in the form of enhanced services.

Collaborating with Cruise Lines
Cruises offer unique travel experiences that combine leisure, adventure, and convenience, making them a popular choice for many travelers. As a travel agent, working with cruise lines allows you to offer your clients a variety of options, ranging from luxury cruises to family-friendly voyages.

Building relationships with cruise lines enables you to access special promotions, discounted rates, and onboard credits that can enhance the overall value of your clients' trips. Cruise lines often have dedicated travel agent programs that provide training, marketing materials, and exclusive offers to help agents sell their products more effectively.

Additionally, cruise lines may offer you the opportunity to experience their services firsthand through fam (familiarization) trips. These trips allow you to explore the ship, experience the onboard activities, and visit the ports of call, giving you valuable firsthand knowledge that you can share with your clients. This in-depth understanding of the cruise experience helps you make tailored recommendations that align with your clients' preferences.

Working closely with cruise lines also means staying updated on new itineraries, ships, and services, ensuring that you can offer your clients the latest and best options available. By aligning your agency with reputable cruise lines, you can establish yourself as a trusted resource for clients seeking memorable and hassle-free cruise vacations.

Car Rental Companies
While airlines and hotels play a significant role in the travel industry, car rental services are also an essential component of many travel experiences, particularly for clients embarking on road trips or visiting remote destinations. Building partnerships with car rental companies allows you to offer clients a variety of transportation options at competitive prices.

Working with reputable car rental companies ensures that your clients receive reliable vehicles and excellent customer service. In return, car rental companies benefit from your referrals and continued business. Car rental companies often provide travel agents with special rates, commissions, and loyalty programs, helping you offer better deals to your clients.

Additionally, building strong relationships with car rental companies enables you to negotiate added perks for your clients, such as complimentary upgrades, GPS units, or unlimited mileage. Offering these extra benefits can make your agency stand out and enhance client satisfaction.

Collaborating with Tour Operators

Tour operators are indispensable in the travel industry, playing a vital role in organizing and executing comprehensive travel packages. These packages typically encompass all facets of a trip, including transportation, accommodations, meals, and guided tours. By collaborating with tour operators, travel agencies can offer clients all-inclusive travel experiences that not only simplify the planning process but also ensure that the itineraries are expertly curated. This not only alleviates the stress of travel planning for clients but also enhances their overall experience, allowing them to focus on enjoying their journey rather than worrying about logistics.

When establishing relationships with tour operators, it is essential to partner with companies that align with your agency's values and cater to the preferences of your clients. For instance, if your clientele consists of eco-conscious travelers, collaborating with a tour operator that specializes in sustainable tourism can significantly enhance the value of your offerings. Such partnerships not only resonate with the interests of your clients but also demonstrate your agency's commitment to responsible travel. This alignment helps build trust and credibility with your clients, reinforcing their decision to choose your agency for their travel needs.

Strong partnerships with tour operators also provide access to exclusive group rates, discounts, and customized tour packages. These advantages can significantly enhance the travel experience for your clients while simultaneously benefiting your agency. For instance, by offering exclusive group rates, you can create enticing package deals that attract more clients and encourage group travel. Customized tour packages allow you to cater to specific interests, whether it's a gourmet food tour, a cultural exploration, or an adventure-filled journey. This level of personalization not only enriches the travel experience but also distinguishes your agency in a competitive market.

Moreover, tour operators typically provide travel agents with commission-based pricing structures, which can help boost your agency's profitability. This commission model enables you to offer clients attractive, well-organized travel experiences while ensuring that your agency remains financially viable. By negotiating favorable commission rates with tour operators, you can maximize your earnings while delivering value to your clients. This symbiotic relationship ultimately enhances your agency's reputation and encourages client loyalty.

Forming strong partnerships with tour operators is essential for any travel agency seeking to provide comprehensive and high-quality travel experiences. By offering all-inclusive packages, aligning with the values of your clients, and leveraging exclusive rates and commissions, your agency can significantly enhance its service offerings and profitability. This collaborative approach not only simplifies the travel planning process for clients but also positions your agency as a go-to source for exceptional travel experiences, ultimately leading to satisfied customers and repeat business.

By maintaining open communication with tour operators and staying up-to-date on their latest offerings, you can provide your clients with unique and tailored travel packages that enhance their overall experience.

Developing a Global Network
The world of travel is vast and diverse, and to truly provide exceptional service to your clients, it's essential to develop a global network of contacts. Having access to local resources, including tour guides, travel bloggers, and destination experts, allows you to offer personalized recommendations, insider knowledge, and

unique experiences that go beyond the standard tourist attractions.

Building Connections with Local Tour Guides
One of the most valuable assets you can offer your clients is access to knowledgeable local tour guides. These individuals are experts in their respective regions and can provide insights into the culture, history, and hidden gems of a destination that your clients might otherwise miss. Whether your clients are interested in exploring the backstreets of Rome, hiking in the Andes, or experiencing the culinary delights of Tokyo, having a trusted local guide can elevate their travel experience.

To build relationships with local tour guides, start by researching reputable guide services in popular destinations. Reach out to guides who have excellent reviews and a proven track record of providing top-notch service. In some cases, you may want to work with tour operators who employ or contract local guides, as this can streamline the booking process.

Another effective way to develop connections with local guides is by attending travel trade shows or joining professional associations. These events provide opportunities to meet guides in person and establish direct relationships. Additionally, collaborating with local tourism boards can help you identify qualified guides and other valuable resources.

By building a network of trusted local tour guides, you can offer your clients enriching experiences that go beyond the standard tourist itinerary. This personalized touch will set your agency apart and help build long-term client loyalty.

Partnering with Travel Bloggers and Influencers

In today's digital age, travel bloggers and influencers play a significant role in shaping the travel decisions of millions of people. These individuals often have large followings on social media platforms and offer insights into destinations, activities, and experiences that may not be widely known.

Partnering with travel bloggers and influencers can help you expand your agency's reach and provide clients with curated recommendations based on firsthand experiences. For example, if a travel blogger has recently visited a destination that your client is interested in, their blog posts, videos, and social media updates can offer valuable insights into the best places to stay, eat, and explore.

To build relationships with travel bloggers and influencers, start by identifying individuals who align with your agency's brand and values. Reach out to them through social media or email, offering to collaborate on content, guest posts, or social media takeovers. Many travel bloggers and influencers are open to partnerships with travel agencies, especially if you can offer them unique experiences or exclusive access to destinations.

By leveraging the influence of travel bloggers and their digital presence, you can enhance your agency's reputation and attract new clients who are seeking authentic, well-informed travel advice.

Connecting with Destination Experts
In addition to local tour guides and influencers, destination experts play a critical role in providing clients with in-depth knowledge of specific regions. These experts may include historians, cultural anthropologists, or professionals in fields such as wildlife conservation, culinary arts, or adventure sports. Connecting with destination experts allows you to offer your clients specialized travel experiences that are tailored to their interests.

For example, if you have a client interested in birdwatching, partnering with a wildlife expert in Costa Rica could result in a customized itinerary that includes guided birdwatching tours in biodiversity hotspots. Alternatively, if your client is a foodie, working with a local chef or culinary expert in Italy could lead to a memorable cooking class or food tour.

Building a network of destination experts requires proactive outreach and relationship-building. Attend travel industry conferences, connect with professionals in your areas of interest, and stay informed about new developments in the regions you serve. By offering clients access to specialized knowledge and experiences, you can create unforgettable trips that cater to their unique interests.

Negotiating Commission and Compensation Models

The financial health of your travel agency depends heavily on the commission and compensation models you negotiate with your suppliers. These agreements directly impact your revenue, profitability, and ability to offer competitive pricing to your clients. To optimize your agency's earnings, it's crucial to understand different pricing structures and negotiate favorable terms with your suppliers.

Commission-Based Pricing
One of the most common compensation models in the travel industry is commission-based pricing. In this model, you earn a percentage of the total booking value from the supplier. The commission rates can vary depending on the supplier and the volume of bookings you generate. For example, airlines, hotels, and cruise lines typically offer commissions ranging from 5% to 15%, depending on the nature of the booking and your agency's relationship with the supplier.

When negotiating commission rates, aim for the highest possible percentage while considering the volume of business you can offer the supplier. Suppliers are often willing to increase commission rates for agencies that consistently generate high-value bookings or demonstrate long-term loyalty.

It's also essential to clarify the payment terms associated with commission-based pricing. Some suppliers pay commissions immediately after the booking is confirmed, while others may pay only after the client has completed their trip. Understanding the payment schedule ensures you can manage your agency's cash flow effectively.

Net Pricing
Net pricing is another compensation model used in the travel industry, particularly for group bookings, customized travel packages, and high-end services. In this model, the supplier provides you with a net price for their services, and you add your markup to determine the final price paid by the client. This pricing model gives you greater flexibility in setting your rates and allows you to increase your profit margins by adjusting the markup based on the complexity and value of the services provided.

Negotiating net pricing agreements requires a deep understanding of the services being offered and the market conditions in which you operate. You'll need to strike a balance between offering competitive pricing to clients and ensuring that your markup is sufficient to cover your operational costs and generate profit.

When negotiating net pricing agreements, it's also essential to clarify any additional fees or surcharges that may apply, such as taxes, service charges, or cancellation penalties. Ensuring transparency in pricing helps build trust with clients and prevents disputes later in the booking process.

Incentive Programs and Bonuses
In addition to commission-based pricing and net pricing, many suppliers offer incentive programs or bonuses for travel agents who meet specific sales targets. These incentives can include cash bonuses, free trips, upgrades, or exclusive access to special promotions. Participating in incentive programs can help boost your agency's revenue and provide added value to your clients.

When negotiating with suppliers, inquire about their incentive programs and how your agency can qualify. Some programs may require you to meet a certain number of bookings within a specific timeframe, while others may be tied to promoting a particular product or destination. Aligning your agency's goals with the supplier's incentive programs can create a win-win situation where both parties benefit from increased sales and customer satisfaction.

Building strong partnerships and maintaining healthy supplier relationships are essential for the long-term success of any travel agency. By collaborating with airlines, hotels, cruise lines, car rental companies, and tour operators, you gain access to exclusive deals, insider knowledge, and valuable resources that enhance the quality of service you offer your clients. Additionally, developing a global network of contacts, including local tour guides, travel bloggers, and destination experts, allows you to provide personalized recommendations and unique travel experiences that set your agency apart from the competition.

Finally, understanding and negotiating favorable commission and compensation models ensure that your agency remains financially sustainable and profitable. By mastering these aspects of supplier relationships, you can position your travel agency as a trusted and reliable partner for both clients and suppliers, paving the way for continued growth and success in the dynamic travel industry.

Chapter 6:
Creating a Marketing Strategy

Marketing is a fundamental aspect of any successful travel agency. A well-thought-out marketing strategy not only helps you attract potential clients but also allows you to communicate your unique value proposition, foster relationships with travelers, and drive consistent bookings. In this chapter, we'll delve deep into the core components of creating an effective marketing strategy for your travel agency. We will explore how to build your brand, design a user-friendly website, leverage social media and content marketing, and invest in paid advertising and SEO to maximize your agency's visibility and growth.

Building Your Brand

Your brand is the cornerstone of your travel agency's identity. It's more than just a logo or a catchy tagline—it's the perception your target audience has of your agency. A strong brand differentiates you from competitors and helps establish credibility and trust. Therefore, when building your brand, focus on creating an identity that resonates with your target market and reflects the values of your business.

Before you design a logo or choose brand colors, start by defining your brand identity. Think about your agency's mission, values, and the emotions you want to evoke in your customers. Are you focused on luxury travel, adventure travel, family vacations, or eco-friendly trips? Your niche will play a significant role in how you position your brand. Once you define this, you can align your branding with the personality of your agency.

For instance, a travel agency focused on eco-tourism might use earthy tones like green and brown, while a luxury travel agency might opt for sleek black and gold to evoke a sense of elegance and sophistication. Additionally, your brand's messaging should reflect its values. If you prioritize customer service, sustainability, or unique experiences, make sure that your slogans, taglines, and communication convey those qualities consistently.

Creating a Logo
Your logo is often the first impression people will have of your brand. It should be visually appealing, simple, and memorable. A well-designed logo becomes a symbol of trust and reliability for clients. When designing your logo, keep in mind that it will be used across multiple platforms, including your website, social media, business cards, and promotional materials. The logo needs to look good in various sizes and formats.

Collaborating with a professional designer can ensure that you create a high-quality, versatile logo. However, if you're on a budget, there are also online tools and platforms where you can design a logo yourself. Just make sure it reflects your brand's identity and aligns with the overall aesthetic of your agency.

Choosing Brand Colors and Fonts
Colors evoke specific emotions and can significantly influence how people perceive your brand. When choosing your brand colors, consider how they relate to your target market. For example, blue is often associated with trust and professionalism, making it a popular choice for travel agencies that want to convey reliability. Meanwhile, vibrant colors like orange and yellow can evoke feelings of adventure and excitement, perfect for agencies catering to thrill-seekers or younger audiences.

Fonts are another important element of your brand's visual identity. Choose a font that complements your logo and aligns with the personality of your brand. A modern sans-serif font might be ideal for an agency specializing in cutting-edge travel experiences, while a more traditional serif font could work well for a classic, luxury travel brand.

Brand Messaging
Once you've defined your visual identity, it's time to work on your brand messaging. This includes your tagline, voice, and overall communication style. Your messaging should reflect your unique value proposition and connect emotionally with your audience. Be consistent with your tone of voice, whether it's formal and professional or friendly and conversational. Use storytelling techniques to showcase the experiences your clients can expect when they choose your agency. By crafting compelling narratives about the trips you offer, you create an emotional connection that can inspire travelers to book with you.

Remember, your brand is more than just a logo—it's an experience that communicates your agency's values and promise to clients. Keep this in mind when building your brand, and ensure that every piece of content or communication from your agency reinforces your identity.

Designing a User-Friendly Website

In today's digital-first world, your website is the virtual storefront of your travel agency. It's often the first point of contact potential clients will have with your business, and as such, it needs to be professional, easy to navigate, and designed to convert visitors into bookings. A well-designed website not only looks aesthetically pleasing but also provides an exceptional user experience that encourages clients to explore your offerings and make travel arrangements through your agency.

Prioritizing User Experience (UX)
A user-friendly website prioritizes ease of use and functionality. When visitors land on your site, they should immediately

understand what your agency offers and how to navigate to the services they're interested in. Your website's layout should be intuitive, with a clear structure that guides users seamlessly through the pages. Ensure that essential information like destination packages, pricing, and booking forms are easy to find.

Additionally, the website must be mobile-friendly. More and more people are browsing the internet and making purchases on their mobile devices, so your site needs to adapt to different screen sizes. A responsive design that automatically adjusts to mobile, tablet, and desktop screens will help you capture clients no matter what device they use.

Engaging Design and Visual Appeal
Visual appeal is critical for a travel agency website. High-quality images of stunning destinations can captivate visitors and spark their wanderlust. Invest in professional photography or use high-resolution images that showcase the types of travel experiences you offer. Whether it's picturesque beaches, thrilling adventure tours, or luxurious hotel stays, your visuals should reflect the unique offerings of your agency.

In addition to beautiful images, ensure your site's design aligns with your brand. The colors, fonts, and overall aesthetic should be consistent with the branding elements you've developed. Striking a balance between elegance and simplicity is key—your design should be clean and clutter-free, allowing users to focus on the content without feeling overwhelmed.

Incorporating Booking Functionality
Your website should include an easy-to-use booking engine that allows clients to reserve their trips directly online. The booking process should be straightforward and user-friendly, with clear instructions and minimal steps. Ensure that clients can easily search

for available packages, choose dates, and complete payments securely.

Integrating secure payment options is also essential. Offer a variety of payment methods, such as credit card, PayPal, and other trusted platforms, to cater to different preferences. Be transparent about pricing and fees, and provide clear confirmation of bookings.

Additional Features: Blogs, Testimonials, and Guides

Enhance your website's value by incorporating additional features like a travel blog, client testimonials, and destination guides. A blog allows you to share your expertise, provide travel tips, and highlight destinations or experiences that align with your agency's niche. Regularly updated blog content not only engages visitors but also helps improve your website's search engine ranking (SEO).

Client testimonials and reviews build trust and provide social proof that reassures potential clients. Include quotes or videos from satisfied customers who have had positive experiences with your agency. Testimonials give credibility to your agency and can persuade hesitant visitors to take the next step and book with you.

Destination guides are another valuable feature that can enhance user experience. Provide detailed information about the places you specialize in, including travel tips, cultural insights, and must-see attractions. These guides position you as an expert in your field and help travelers make informed decisions when planning their trips.

Search Engine Optimization (SEO) Best Practices

Your website needs to be easily discoverable by search engines like Google to attract organic traffic. SEO involves optimizing your website's content and structure to improve its ranking in search results. This means using relevant keywords, optimizing page load speed, and ensuring your site is mobile-friendly.

Keyword research is a crucial part of SEO. Identify the phrases and terms your target audience is likely to search for and incorporate them naturally into your website content. This could include terms like "luxury travel packages," "eco-friendly vacations," or "adventure tours in Asia." By strategically placing these keywords in your titles, headings, and descriptions, you increase the likelihood of ranking higher in search results.

Additionally, consider implementing technical SEO strategies such as optimizing meta descriptions, using descriptive alt tags for images, and improving internal linking. A well-optimized website will attract more visitors and increase the chances of converting them into paying clients.

Social Media and Content Marketing

Social media has revolutionized how businesses interact with customers, and travel agencies are no exception. By leveraging social media platforms like Instagram, Facebook, and Pinterest, you can engage with potential clients, showcase your expertise, and promote your destination packages. Social media not only helps you build an online presence but also serves as a powerful tool for inspiring wanderlust and driving bookings.

Choosing the Right Social Media Platforms
Each social media platform presents unique opportunities for travel agencies to reach and engage their target audience effectively. Understanding the strengths of each platform can help you tailor your marketing strategies based on your niche and clientele.

Instagram: As a platform renowned for its visual appeal, Instagram is particularly well-suited for travel agencies looking to showcase stunning destinations and memorable experiences. High-quality photos and videos can capture the essence of a location, inspiring potential travelers to book their next adventure. Instagram Stories and Reels are excellent tools for providing a behind-the-scenes look at your trips, sharing tips, and highlighting special promotions or travel deals. The platform's emphasis on aesthetics also allows for creative storytelling, which can evoke emotions and create a strong desire for travel among your audience. Utilizing relevant hashtags can further enhance your reach, enabling you to connect with like-minded travelers and build a loyal following.

Facebook: With its diverse user base, Facebook offers travel agencies a platform to connect with a wide audience. It is ideal for sharing longer-form content, such as blog posts or travel guides, which can provide in-depth information about destinations, travel tips, and agency services. The interactive nature of Facebook allows for meaningful engagement through comments, direct messages, and sharing user-generated content. Additionally, creating and managing Facebook groups can foster a sense of community around specific travel interests, where members can share experiences, ask questions, and receive recommendations. This engagement not only helps build brand loyalty but also positions your agency as a trusted source of travel information.

Pinterest: Often described as a visual search engine, Pinterest is an excellent platform for travel agencies seeking to inspire potential travelers. Users turn to Pinterest for ideas and inspiration, making it a valuable space for showcasing destinations, itineraries, and travel tips. By creating boards dedicated to various themes—such as adventure travel, luxury getaways, or family vacations—you can attract users actively searching for their next vacation. Each pin serves as a gateway to your content, directing users to your website or blog for further exploration. Pinterest's algorithm promotes evergreen content, meaning your pins can continue to generate traffic long after they are posted, making it a cost-effective tool for long-term audience engagement.

By leveraging the unique strengths of Instagram, Facebook, and Pinterest, travel agencies can craft targeted marketing strategies that resonate with their audience. Understanding where your ideal clients spend their time online will allow you to focus your efforts on the platforms that are most likely to yield positive results.

Creating Engaging Content
The key to success on social media is creating content that resonates with your audience. Focus on producing high-quality, visually appealing posts that showcase your agency's expertise and the unique experiences you offer. Share destination photos, travel itineraries, behind-the-scenes footage, and customer testimonials. Engage with your audience by responding to comments and encouraging them to share their own travel experiences.

Storytelling is a powerful way to connect emotionally with potential clients. Share stories about your travelers' experiences, highlighting the moments that made their trips special. Use captions to provide context for your visuals, offer travel tips, or share interesting facts about the destinations you specialize in. The goal is to inspire your audience and encourage them to dream about their next vacation—hopefully with your agency.

Leveraging Influencers and Partnerships
Influencer marketing is another effective way to reach a broader audience. Partner with travel bloggers, influencers, or social media personalities who align with your brand and niche. Influencers can help promote your agency to their followers through sponsored posts, travel collaborations, or destination takeovers. By leveraging their established trust with their audience, you can build credibility and increase brand awareness.

Similarly, partnerships with other businesses in the travel industry—such as hotels, airlines, or local tour operators—can help expand your reach. Collaborate on social media campaigns, offer joint promotions, or co-create content that highlights both of your offerings.

User-Generated Content
User-generated content (UGC) is a valuable resource for travel agencies. Encourage your clients to share their travel experiences on social media and tag your agency in their posts. Repost their content on your own channels to showcase real travelers enjoying trips arranged by your agency. UGC builds social proof and authenticity, showing potential clients that others have had positive experiences with your agency.

You can also run social media contests or campaigns that invite your audience to share their travel stories or photos for a chance to be featured on your page. This not only increases engagement but also provides you with fresh content to share with your followers.

Measuring Social Media Success
To ensure your social media efforts are effective, track and measure your results. Most social media platforms offer built-in analytics tools that allow you to monitor engagement metrics such as likes, shares, comments, and followers. Analyze which types of content perform best and adjust your strategy accordingly. For example, if Instagram Reels generate more engagement than static posts, focus on creating more video content.

In addition to engagement metrics, track website traffic and bookings generated from social media. Use tools like Google Analytics to see how social media referrals contribute to your overall sales. By continuously analyzing your performance, you can optimize your social media strategy and maximize your return on investment (ROI).

Paid Advertising and SEO

To further amplify your online presence and attract more clients, paid advertising and search engine optimization (SEO) are essential components of a comprehensive marketing strategy. Both of these tactics can help drive traffic to your website, increase brand visibility, and ultimately boost bookings.

Paid Advertising

Paid advertising allows you to target specific demographics and audiences with tailored campaigns. Platforms like Google Ads, Facebook Ads, and Instagram promotions offer various options for running targeted ads that reach people based on their location, interests, and online behavior. Here's how you can make the most of paid advertising:

Google Ads: Google Ads is an effective way to capture potential clients who are actively searching for travel-related services. By bidding on relevant keywords, your agency's ads can appear at the top of search results when users search for terms like "best vacation packages" or "luxury travel deals." Google Ads operates on a pay-per-click (PPC) model, meaning you only pay when someone clicks on your ad. The key to success with Google Ads is choosing the right keywords, creating compelling ad copy, and optimizing your campaigns to ensure high-quality leads.

Facebook and Instagram Ads: Facebook and Instagram offer a wide range of ad formats, including image ads, video ads, carousel ads, and Stories ads. You can use these platforms to target specific audiences based on their demographics, interests, and behaviors. For instance, you can create an ad campaign targeting people interested in adventure travel or eco-tourism. Facebook's robust targeting capabilities make it easy to reach the right audience and drive traffic to your website or landing pages.

Remarketing
Remarketing, also known as retargeting, is a highly effective form of paid advertising that targets users who have already visited your website or engaged with your content. By showing targeted ads to users who have shown interest in your services but haven't yet made a booking, you can remind them of your offerings and encourage them to return and complete the booking process. Remarketing ads often have higher conversion rates since they target users who are already familiar with your brand.

Search Engine Optimization (SEO)
While paid ads can provide immediate visibility, SEO is a long-term strategy that helps improve your website's ranking in organic search results. By optimizing your website for search engines like Google, you increase the likelihood of attracting visitors who are searching for travel services.

On-Page SEO
On-page SEO involves optimizing the content and structure of your website to make it more search-engine-friendly. This includes:

Keyword Research: Identify the search terms and phrases your potential clients are using when looking for travel services. Use tools like Google Keyword Planner or SEMrush to find relevant keywords and incorporate them into your website content, meta descriptions, and headers.

Content Optimization: Create high-quality, informative content that answers common questions or provides valuable insights about travel destinations, tips, or experiences. The more helpful your content is to users, the more likely it is to rank higher in search results. For example, a blog post titled "Top 10 Adventure Destinations in South America" can attract users interested in adventure travel, while also incorporating relevant keywords for SEO.

Technical SEO: Ensure that your website is technically optimized for search engines. This includes improving page load speed, ensuring mobile-friendliness, and creating a clear site structure with internal links. Use descriptive alt tags for images and make sure your website's URLs are SEO-friendly.

Off-Page SEO
Off-page SEO refers to external factors that influence your website's ranking, such as backlinks and social signals. Building high-quality backlinks from reputable websites in the travel industry can boost your site's authority and improve its ranking in search results.

Local SEO
If your travel agency caters to specific geographic areas, local SEO is essential. This involves optimizing your website for location-based searches, such as "travel agency in New York" or "luxury vacations in California." Create a Google My Business profile to ensure your agency appears in local search results, and encourage satisfied clients to leave positive reviews to boost your online reputation.

Creating a marketing strategy for your travel agency involves a multi-faceted approach that includes branding, web design, social media marketing, paid advertising, and SEO. By building a strong brand, designing an engaging and functional website, leveraging social media platforms, and investing in paid and organic marketing strategies, you can significantly enhance your agency's visibility and attract a loyal client base.

Marketing is an ongoing process that requires constant analysis, adaptation, and optimization. By staying on top of industry trends, listening to your audience, and refining your strategy based on data and performance metrics, you can ensure your travel agency remains competitive in an ever-changing market.

Chapter 7:
Managing Operations and Customer Experience

In the travel industry, managing operations and ensuring an exceptional customer experience are critical to the success of your agency. Efficient systems, strong customer service, and the ability to manage challenges and emergencies define the quality of service you provide and, ultimately, your reputation. In this chapter, we will delve into the essential aspects of managing operations and providing a seamless customer experience, from booking systems and software to handling complaints and emergencies. These areas form the backbone of a successful travel agency and are crucial for fostering client trust, retention, and satisfaction.

Booking Systems and Software

In today's digital age, investing in an efficient and reliable booking system is one of the most important decisions you can make for your travel agency. A well-designed booking system can streamline operations, enhance the client experience, and improve overall business efficiency. Managing multiple client bookings, tracking payments, and handling reservations manually can be overwhelming and time-consuming. That's where modern booking systems and software solutions come in to simplify these processes.

A travel booking system serves as the operational heart of your agency. It allows you to manage client bookings from the initial inquiry all the way to trip completion. By integrating various functions such as payment tracking, reservation management, and client communications, booking software eliminates much of the administrative burden, leaving you with more time to focus on enhancing customer service and growing your business.

When selecting a booking system, consider features that align with your agency's specific needs. For instance, if your agency specializes in organizing group tours, look for a system that allows for the management of multiple reservations under one booking. Alternatively, if you focus on individual luxury travelers, you might require a system that offers customization options to tailor trips to specific client preferences.

A robust booking system should offer the following features:

Real-time Availability and Reservations: Real-time booking ensures that availability is up-to-date, preventing double bookings or overbookings. It also allows clients to check available dates and services instantly, improving the booking experience.

Payment Processing and Tracking: Integrated payment systems allow clients to pay for their trips securely through your platform. Automatic payment tracking helps you keep tabs on what has been paid and what is outstanding, reducing the risk of missed or delayed payments.

Automated Confirmation and Reminders: Sending automated booking confirmations and reminders can help keep clients informed and reduce the chance of missed or forgotten bookings. Reminders can also serve to upsell additional services, such as optional excursions or travel insurance.

Customization and Flexibility: Clients expect flexibility in their travel plans. A booking system should allow you to adjust itineraries, add or remove services, and handle special requests without needing to start the booking process from scratch.

Reporting and Analytics: Access to detailed reporting on bookings, revenue, and customer demographics is invaluable for tracking your agency's performance and making informed business decisions.

Beyond booking software, it's also essential to invest in Customer Relationship Management (CRM) software to manage your client interactions and keep track of individual preferences. A CRM system enables you to maintain a detailed history of each client, including past trips, favorite destinations, preferred travel styles, and any special needs or requests. This data allows you to personalize your services and marketing efforts, making clients feel valued and understood. Moreover, CRM systems help with follow-up communications, such as post-trip surveys, special offers, or birthday greetings, which further enhance client loyalty.

CRM software can also improve operational efficiency by automating routine tasks like sending out emails or creating reminders to follow up with clients after their trips. Furthermore, by analyzing customer data, you can gain insights into your client base, such as identifying trends in travel preferences or pinpointing opportunities to upsell or cross-sell additional services.

For smaller agencies, there are affordable, user-friendly CRM options available that integrate well with most booking systems. Larger agencies may benefit from more advanced solutions with customizable features and higher levels of automation. Ultimately, your choice of CRM should align with your agency's goals and scale.

An efficient booking system combined with CRM software not only enhances your internal operations but also contributes to an improved client experience. Streamlined operations mean faster response times, fewer errors, and a higher level of service, all of which contribute to client satisfaction and loyalty.

Providing Excellent Customer Service

Exceptional customer service is the foundation of a successful travel agency. In an industry where word-of-mouth referrals and repeat business are vital, ensuring that every client feels valued and cared for can significantly impact your agency's reputation and success. Providing outstanding customer service goes beyond simply answering questions or making bookings; it involves building lasting relationships with your clients and ensuring their entire experience, from inquiry to post-trip follow-up, is seamless.

The first step to delivering excellent customer service is ensuring that your team is well-trained and understands the importance of client care. Customer service in the travel industry involves more than just basic politeness; it requires empathy, problem-solving skills, and a proactive attitude. Clients rely on travel agents to guide them through what can often be a complex and stressful process, whether it's booking flights, finding accommodation, or planning activities. Your role is to make this process as smooth and enjoyable as possible.

Personalization is a key element of great customer service. Today's travelers expect more than cookie-cutter itineraries; they want experiences tailored to their preferences and needs. Whether it's recommending a quiet beach for a family looking to relax or suggesting an adventurous hike for thrill-seekers, understanding and catering to each client's unique preferences is crucial. Use the data collected in your CRM system to offer personalized recommendations, create customized travel itineraries, and send tailored offers based on previous bookings.

Communication plays a central role in customer service. Responding promptly to inquiries, keeping clients informed at every stage of the booking process, and following up after the trip are essential to maintaining client satisfaction. Clients should feel confident that they can reach you whenever they need assistance, whether before, during, or after their trip. Offering multiple communication channels—such as phone, email, chat, and social media—ensures that clients can contact you in the way that is most convenient for them.

Another aspect of excellent customer service is setting clear expectations. Clients need to know exactly what is included in their travel package, any potential additional costs, and what to expect during their trip. Being upfront about cancellation policies, refund options, and any travel restrictions will prevent misunderstandings and ensure that clients are fully informed before they book.

In addition to clarity and communication, it's important to go the extra mile to exceed client expectations. Small gestures, such as providing travel tips, arranging for special amenities at their hotel, or sending a personalized thank-you note after their trip, can leave a lasting impression and encourage repeat business.

Post-trip follow-ups are another vital component of customer service. Once a client returns from their trip, send a follow-up message to thank them for choosing your agency and to ask for feedback. Not only does this show that you value their opinion, but it also provides valuable insights into areas where you can improve. Positive feedback can be used for testimonials or reviews, while constructive criticism can help you refine your services and address any issues before they impact future bookings.

Lastly, loyalty programs or incentives for repeat customers can also enhance customer retention. Offering discounts, exclusive offers, or priority booking to loyal clients shows that you appreciate their business and encourages them to return for future trips.

In summary, providing excellent customer service is about creating an experience that leaves clients feeling supported, understood, and valued throughout their entire travel journey. From personalized service to clear communication and thoughtful follow-ups, focusing on the client experience will help you build strong relationships, encourage repeat business, and generate positive word-of-mouth referrals.

Handling Complaints and Emergencies

No matter how carefully you plan or how well you manage your agency's operations, travel is inherently unpredictable, and things don't always go according to plan. Flights can be delayed, accommodations may not meet expectations, and emergencies can arise. How you handle complaints and emergencies can make a significant difference in maintaining client satisfaction and protecting your agency's reputation.

First and foremost, it is essential to have a protocol in place for managing complaints and emergencies. A well-defined process will ensure that you and your team are prepared to handle issues quickly and professionally, minimizing disruption to the client's travel experience and reducing the likelihood of negative reviews or lost business.

When dealing with client complaints, the first step is to listen carefully to the issue at hand. Clients want to feel heard, and by actively listening, you can better understand their concerns and take appropriate action. Sometimes, clients simply want to vent their frustrations, and offering a sympathetic ear can go a long way in diffusing a tense situation.

Once you understand the problem, take ownership of the issue. Even if the problem was caused by a third-party supplier, such as an airline or hotel, clients will still hold your agency responsible for their overall experience. Acknowledge the issue and take immediate steps to resolve it. If a client's hotel room isn't up to standard, for example, offer to find them alternative accommodations or negotiate a refund with the hotel on their behalf. The key is to act swiftly and show the client that you are committed to resolving the problem.

When it comes to emergency situations, such as natural disasters, medical emergencies, or last-minute cancellations, the ability to act quickly and provide clear guidance is critical. Make sure that you have an emergency response plan in place that includes protocols for various scenarios, such as:

Flight Cancellations or Delays: If a client's flight is canceled or significantly delayed, work to find them alternative travel options as quickly as possible. Stay in contact with the airline and keep the client informed of any updates or changes.

Medical Emergencies: If a client experiences a medical emergency while traveling, assist them in locating medical facilities and arranging for transportation if needed. Ensure that you have contact information for local hospitals or clinics at popular travel destinations, and make sure the client has access to travel insurance that covers medical emergencies.

Natural Disasters or Political Unrest: In the event of a natural disaster or political unrest at a client's destination, communicate with them immediately to ensure their safety. Help them arrange for evacuation if necessary and assist with travel insurance claims.

Last-Minute Cancellations: If a client cancels their trip at the last minute due to unforeseen circumstances, review your cancellation policies and see if any exceptions can be made. Where possible, negotiate with suppliers to minimize cancellation fees or offer a credit for future travel.

In all cases, communication is paramount. Keep clients updated at every stage of the resolution process, and be transparent about what you can and cannot do to rectify the situation. Even if the issue cannot be fully resolved to the client's satisfaction, the fact that you acted quickly and kept them informed can help preserve your agency's reputation.

After handling a complaint or emergency, follow up with the client to ensure that they are satisfied with the outcome. If appropriate, offer a goodwill gesture, such as a discount on a future booking or a complimentary service, to demonstrate that you value their business and want to make amends for the disruption.

Handling complaints and emergencies effectively requires preparation, empathy, and quick thinking. By having a plan in place, staying calm under pressure, and maintaining open lines of communication, you can turn a potentially negative situation into an opportunity to demonstrate your agency's professionalism and commitment to client satisfaction.

Managing operations and ensuring a seamless customer experience are key to running a successful travel agency. By investing in the right booking systems and software, providing excellent customer service, and handling complaints and emergencies effectively, you can create a travel experience that exceeds client expectations and fosters long-term loyalty.

Chapter 8:
Scaling Your Travel Agency

Scaling a travel agency is an exciting yet challenging journey that requires strategic planning, execution, and a strong foundation. As your business grows, new opportunities arise, but so do complexities in managing operations, client expectations, and market competition. In this chapter, we'll explore various facets of scaling your travel agency, from expanding service offerings and hiring the right staff to leveraging technology to drive growth. Successfully scaling your business requires a combination of adaptability, foresight, and continuous improvement. It is a delicate balance of expanding your footprint while maintaining the level of service that helped your agency grow in the first place.

Expanding Your Services

One of the key drivers for growth in any travel agency is the ability to diversify and expand service offerings. As your client base grows and you become more established in the market, expanding into new services or markets can open up fresh revenue streams and help you stay competitive. However, it is important to approach expansion thoughtfully, ensuring that new services align with your brand, customer preferences, and industry trends.

Before deciding to expand your service offerings, it's crucial to assess market demand. This requires conducting thorough market research to identify gaps or opportunities within your niche or the broader travel industry. For instance, if wellness travel is gaining popularity, offering yoga retreats, spa vacations, or mindfulness travel packages could align with emerging trends. Alternatively, if you notice that adventure travel is on the rise, offering more extreme sports or outdoor adventure packages could attract a new segment of clients.

Look closely at your current customer base and consider which additional services could enhance their experience or meet unmet needs. Surveys and feedback forms can provide invaluable insight into what your customers are looking for and help guide your expansion strategy. If your existing clients frequently ask about specific destinations or travel styles, such as eco-tourism or family-oriented vacations, this could indicate potential areas for growth.

Introducing New Destinations
Expanding your range of destinations is a common and effective way to grow your travel agency. By offering new and exciting locations, you not only attract a broader audience but also give your existing customers more reasons to return to your agency for future travel plans. However, it's essential to introduce new destinations strategically. You need to ensure that you have strong partnerships with local service providers, such as hotels, tour operators, and guides, and that you can offer these new locations at competitive prices.

It's also important to consider logistical challenges such as language barriers, safety concerns, and travel regulations. For instance, expanding into remote or less-traveled destinations may require additional research to ensure smooth operations and customer satisfaction.

Group Tours and Special Interest Travel
Another way to scale your agency is by offering specialized travel packages, such as group tours or themed vacations. Group travel can be highly profitable because it allows you to cater to multiple clients simultaneously, creating a shared travel experience that appeals to specific demographics. Group tours can be tailored to different audiences, such as families, solo travelers, seniors, or corporate teams, giving you the flexibility to market your services to diverse customer groups.

Additionally, you can create themed or special-interest travel packages to cater to niche markets. For example, you could offer culinary tours for food enthusiasts, cultural tours for history buffs, or photography tours for amateur photographers. This type of specialized service can set you apart from competitors and position your agency as an expert in a particular type of travel.

Wellness and Adventure Travel
Wellness and adventure travel are two of the fastest-growing segments in the travel industry, and expanding into these areas can give your agency a competitive edge. Wellness travel focuses on physical, mental, and emotional well-being, offering experiences such as yoga retreats, detox programs, meditation workshops, and spa vacations. This type of travel appeals to individuals seeking a break from the stresses of everyday life and offers a rejuvenating, mindful experience.

Adventure travel, on the other hand, attracts thrill-seekers looking for excitement and exploration. Offering packages that include activities such as hiking, mountain climbing, scuba diving, or safari tours can open up a new market of active travelers. To successfully tap into the adventure travel market, it's essential to partner with experienced and certified local guides and ensure that all safety protocols are in place.

Luxury and Bespoke Travel
As your agency grows, you may want to target high-end clients by offering luxury or bespoke travel services. Luxury travel focuses on offering premium experiences, including five-star accommodations, private tours, and exclusive access to events or destinations. Bespoke travel, meanwhile, is highly personalized, with itineraries tailored to meet the specific desires of each client.

These types of services require a high level of attention to detail and excellent relationships with premium service providers.

By diversifying your service offerings and expanding into new areas of travel, you can tap into emerging markets, meet customer demand, and position your agency for long-term growth.

Hiring and Training Staff

As your travel agency expands, it becomes increasingly clear that you can't do everything on your own. Managing a growing client base, multiple service offerings, and operational complexities requires a strong team that shares your vision and values. The quality of your staff is a major factor in determining the success of your agency. From customer service to marketing and operations, every team member plays a crucial role in delivering an exceptional client experience and driving growth.

Building the Right Team
Hiring the right people starts with identifying the roles that are essential for your agency's success. Depending on the size of your agency, you may need to hire staff to manage areas such as operations, customer service, marketing, sales, and finance. Each of these roles requires specific skill sets and experience, and it's important to hire individuals who not only meet the technical qualifications but also align with your agency's brand values and culture.

Operations Staff are responsible for ensuring that all travel bookings, reservations, and logistics run smoothly. They need to be detail-oriented, organized, and capable of handling the fast-paced nature of the travel industry. Operations staff may also handle supplier relationships, negotiate contracts, and ensure that all services meet quality standards.

Customer Service Representatives are the face of your agency. They interact directly with clients, handle inquiries, resolve issues, and ensure that clients have a positive experience throughout their travel journey. Strong communication skills, empathy, and problem-solving abilities are essential for this role.

Marketing and Sales Staff play a critical role in promoting your agency and attracting new clients. They should be well-versed in digital marketing strategies, including social media, content marketing, SEO, and email campaigns. Sales staff need to understand the travel industry and be able to build relationships with potential clients to drive bookings.

Finance and Accounting Staff ensure that your agency's financial operations are running smoothly. They handle billing, payments, budgeting, and financial reporting, ensuring that your agency remains profitable and compliant with tax regulations.

Training and Development
Once you have hired the right team, investing in their training and development is crucial. The travel industry is constantly evolving, and your staff needs to be equipped with the knowledge and skills to stay competitive. Provide comprehensive training on your agency's services, booking systems, and customer service protocols. Additionally, ensure that staff are up-to-date on industry trends, travel regulations, and emerging destinations.

Customer service training should be a top priority, as it directly impacts client satisfaction and retention. Equip your staff with the tools to handle client inquiries, resolve issues, and manage complaints effectively. Role-playing exercises can help staff develop the skills needed to interact with clients in a professional and empathetic manner.

In addition to initial training, ongoing development is important to keep your team motivated and engaged. Offer opportunities for staff to attend industry conferences, webinars, or workshops. Encouraging continuous learning will not only improve their performance but also foster a culture of innovation and growth within your agency.

Creating a Positive Work Environment
A positive work environment is essential for retaining top talent and fostering collaboration. As your agency grows, it's important to create a culture where employees feel valued, supported, and motivated. Encourage open communication, provide regular feedback, and recognize the hard work and achievements of your staff.

Offering competitive compensation packages, including salary, benefits, and bonuses, is essential for attracting and retaining skilled employees. Additionally, offering perks such as flexible working hours, travel discounts, or opportunities for personal travel can make your agency an attractive place to work.

Creating a strong team and investing in their development is essential for scaling your travel agency. As your staff grows, so will your ability to manage more clients, expand services, and deliver a high level of service consistently.

Leveraging Technology for Growth

In today's digital age, technology plays a pivotal role in the growth and success of travel agencies. From streamlining internal operations to enhancing the customer experience, adopting the right technological tools can give your agency a competitive edge and position you for scalable growth. The travel industry is constantly evolving, and agencies that embrace new technologies are better equipped to meet customer expectations, manage operations efficiently, and stay ahead of industry trends.

Embracing Automation
One of the most significant advantages of leveraging technology in the travel industry is the ability to automate routine tasks, freeing up time for your staff to focus on more complex and high-value activities. Automation can be applied in several areas, including:

Booking and Reservations: Automated booking systems allow clients to browse and book trips online, reducing the need for manual input from your staff. Automated confirmation emails, payment reminders, and updates also help keep clients informed and reduce the chance of missed communications.

Payment Processing: Automation tools can streamline the payment process, ensuring that invoices are sent out on time and payments are tracked accurately. Integrated payment systems also allow clients to pay for their trips through secure online portals, reducing the need for manual invoicing.

Client Communication: Chatbots and automated email sequences can handle common client inquiries, such as questions about available packages or booking processes. This frees up customer service representatives to focus on more complex inquiries and allows your agency to provide instant responses to client queries.

Personalization and Data-Driven Insights
Personalization is a key trend in the travel industry, and technology enables agencies to deliver tailored experiences that meet the unique preferences of each client. By leveraging customer data and insights, you can create personalized travel recommendations, offer custom itineraries, and suggest activities or destinations based on a client's travel history and preferences.

Customer relationship management (CRM) software is an essential tool for storing and analyzing client data. A CRM system allows you to track client interactions, preferences, booking histories, and feedback, enabling you to create a more personalized experience for each traveler. For example, if a client frequently books beach vacations, you can send them tailored offers for beach destinations during the holiday season.

Additionally, using data analytics tools can help you identify trends in customer behavior, such as the most popular destinations or travel times. This data can inform your marketing strategies, allowing you to target your audience with offers that are relevant and appealing to them.

Artificial Intelligence and Chatbots
Artificial intelligence (AI) is transforming the travel industry by providing new ways to enhance customer service, streamline operations, and offer personalized experiences. AI-powered chatbots, for example, can handle a wide range of tasks, from answering customer queries to assisting with bookings. These chatbots can operate 24/7, providing clients with immediate responses and reducing the need for human intervention in simple queries.

AI can also be used to predict travel trends, analyze customer feedback, and optimize pricing strategies. Machine learning algorithms can analyze historical data to predict future demand for certain destinations or travel packages, allowing you to make informed decisions about pricing, promotions, and inventory management.

Mobile Apps and Client Portals

Mobile apps and client portals have become essential tools for modern travel agencies. Many travelers now prefer to book trips, access itineraries, and communicate with their travel agents through their smartphones. Developing a user-friendly mobile app or client portal can enhance the customer experience by offering clients easy access to their travel details, booking confirmations, and real-time updates.

A mobile app can also serve as a powerful marketing tool. Through push notifications, you can send personalized offers, destination recommendations, and travel tips directly to your clients' phones. Additionally, integrating social sharing features within your app allows clients to share their travel experiences with friends and family, further promoting your agency through word-of-mouth marketing.

Cloud-Based Solutions
Cloud-based solutions offer a scalable and cost-effective way to manage your travel agency's operations. By storing your data and software on the cloud, you can access your systems from anywhere, allowing for remote work and improved collaboration between team members. Cloud-based booking systems, CRM tools, and project management platforms enable real-time updates and ensure that all team members have access to the same information, no matter where they are located.

Scalability is one of the biggest advantages of cloud-based solutions. As your agency grows, you can easily add new users, increase storage capacity, and integrate additional tools without needing to invest in costly hardware or infrastructure.

Social Media and Digital Marketing
Technology also plays a crucial role in scaling your agency's marketing efforts. Social media platforms like Instagram, Facebook,

and TikTok provide an ideal way to promote your services, share travel inspiration, and connect with potential clients. Visual content, such as photos and videos of destinations, can capture the attention of travelers and encourage them to book trips through your agency.

Investing in digital marketing strategies, such as search engine optimization (SEO), paid advertising, and content marketing, can help you reach a larger audience and drive more traffic to your website. Tools like Google Analytics and social media analytics platforms allow you to track the performance of your marketing campaigns and make data-driven adjustments to optimize your results.

As your agency grows, it's important to have a comprehensive digital marketing strategy that includes a mix of organic and paid tactics. This will ensure that you reach a wide audience and continuously attract new clients.

The Role of Technology in Customer Experience
Technology not only improves operational efficiency but also plays a key role in enhancing the overall customer experience. By adopting user-friendly tools, such as online booking platforms, mobile apps, and automated communication systems, you can create a seamless and enjoyable experience for your clients from the moment they start researching their trip to the time they return home.

For instance, sending automated pre-departure emails with packing tips, destination information, and reminders can help prepare your clients for their trip. Similarly, offering an easy way for clients to access their itineraries, vouchers, and travel documents through a mobile app or client portal adds convenience to the travel experience.

Finally, post-trip follow-up emails or surveys allow you to gather feedback, maintain relationships with your clients, and encourage repeat bookings.

Scaling a travel agency requires a combination of strategic planning, investing in the right technology, building a strong team, and continuously expanding your service offerings. By staying attuned to industry trends, leveraging data to personalize experiences, and adopting tools that streamline operations, you can position your agency for long-term growth and success. As you scale, always remember that maintaining the quality of your service and client relationships is just as important as expanding your reach. Keep your clients at the center of everything you do, and your travel agency will thrive as you continue to grow.

Conclusion

Starting a travel agency requires passion, strategic planning, and continuous learning. The journey to building a thriving travel business is both exciting and challenging, but with a clear vision and a well-defined strategy, success is within reach. Throughout this book, you've been equipped with the foundational steps necessary to turn your dream of owning a travel agency into reality. From understanding the market and establishing your niche to leveraging technology and expanding your service offerings, each step plays a crucial role in setting your business up for growth and long-term success.

Dedication is key when it comes to standing out in a competitive industry like travel. As you grow your agency, staying adaptable and proactive will allow you to respond to shifting market trends and client preferences. Whether it's adopting new technologies, refining your marketing approach, or expanding into new travel segments, being open to innovation is essential. Building a strong reputation through excellent customer service and personalized experiences will set you apart from the competition, fostering long-lasting relationships with your clients.

Moreover, the tools you choose to invest in—whether customer relationship management systems, mobile apps, or marketing platforms—will significantly impact your agency's ability to operate efficiently and scale over time. These tools not only streamline operations but also enhance the overall client experience, which is at the heart of any successful travel business. The ability to provide seamless booking experiences, personalized recommendations, and continuous support will help establish your brand as a trusted resource for travelers.

At the core of every thriving travel agency is a customer-focused approach. The satisfaction and loyalty of your clients are the true indicators of success. As you continue to grow your business, always prioritize the needs and desires of your clients. By offering memorable travel experiences and exceptional service, you can inspire loyalty and encourage repeat bookings, helping your business thrive in the long term.

With dedication, the right tools, and a focus on providing value to your clients, you are well on your way to building a successful travel business that helps people explore the world and create lasting memories. This book has given you the roadmap to navigate the complex and rewarding journey of entrepreneurship in the travel industry. With passion and persistence, the possibilities for your agency's growth are limitless.

Made in the USA
Las Vegas, NV
31 January 2025

17315343R10066